Nonprofit Marketing

John L. Fortenberry, Jr., MBA, PhD, PhD

Chair, James K. Elrod Department of Health
Administration

MHA Program Director

James K. Elrod Professor of Health Administration

Professor of Marketing

School of Business

LSU Shreveport

Shreveport, Louisiana

JONES & BARTLETT
LEARNING

World Headquarters
Jones & Bartlett Learning
5 Wall Street
Burlington, MA 01803
978-443-5000
info@jblearning.com
www.jblearning.com

Jones & Bartlett Learning books and products are available through most bookstores and online book-sellers. To contact Jones & Bartlett Learning directly, call 800-832-0034, fax 978-443-8000, or visit our website, www.jblearning.com.

Substantial discounts on bulk quantities of Jones & Bartlett Learning publications are available to corporations, professional associations, and other qualified organizations. For details and specific discount information, contact the special sales department at Jones & Bartlett Learning via the above contact information or send an email to specialsales@jblearning.com.

This publication is designed to provide accurate and authoritative information in regard to the Subject Matter covered. It is sold with the understanding that the publisher is not engaged in rendering legal, accounting, or other professional service. If legal advice or other expert assistance is required, the service of a competent professional person should be sought.

Production Credits
Publisher: Michael Brown
Editorial Assistant: Chloe Falivene
Production Manager: Tracey McCrea
Senior Marketing Manager: Sophie Fleck Teague
Manufacturing and Inventory Control Supervisor: Amy Bacus
Composition: Cenveo Publisher Services
Cover Design: Timothy Dziewit
Cover Image: © Transfuchsian/ShutterStock, Inc.
Printing and Binding: Edwards Brothers Malloy
Cover Printing: Edwards Brothers Malloy

Library of Congress Cataloging-in-Publication Data

Fortenberry, John L.
  Nonprofit marketing / John Fortenberry.
    p. cm.
  Includes bibliographical references and index.
  ISBN 978-0-7637-8261-0 (pbk.)
1. Nonprofit organizations—Marketing. 2. Marketing. 3. New products. I. Title.
  HF5415.F5668 2013
  658.8—dc23
                          2011037935

6048
Printed in the United States of America
16 15 14 13 12   10 9 8 7 6 5 4 3 2 1

In Memory of my Father
Dr. John Lamar Fortenberry
1922–2005

Acknowledgments

A special note of thanks is extended to Michael Brown, Maro Gartside, and the rest of the Jones & Bartlett Learning team for their helpful guidance and support throughout the development, publication, and promotion of this text. Their assistance permitted *Nonprofit Marketing* to become a reality.

About the Author

John L. Fortenberry, Jr. serves as chair of the James K. Elrod Department of Health Administration, MHA program director, James K. Elrod Professor of Health Administration, and professor of marketing in the School of Business at LSU Shreveport, where he teaches a variety of courses in both health administration and marketing.

He received a BBA in marketing from the University of Mississippi; an MBA from Mississippi College; a PhD in public administration and public policy, with concentrations in health administration, human resource management, and organization theory, from Auburn University; and a PhD in business administration, with a major in marketing, from the University of Manchester in the United Kingdom.

Dr. Fortenberry's academic research interests are centered on marketing, including the components of advertising, consumer behavior, and strategy. His specific sector interests include health, retail, and transportation industries. He is the author of six books, including *Health Care Marketing: Tools and Techniques*, published by Jones & Bartlett Learning.

Contents

Values-Driven Leadership 223
Strategic Focus 223
Executional Excellence 224
Control of Destiny 224
Trust-Based Relationships 224
Investment in Employee Success 225
Acting Small 225
Brand Cultivation 225
Generosity 226
Operational Matters 226
Summary 226
Exercises 227
Reference 227

Chapter 32   George Day's Market Orientation Model 229
Learning Objectives 229
Introduction 229
Culture 231
Capabilities 232
Configuration 232
Operational Matters 233
Summary 233
Exercises 233
Reference 234

Chapter 33   Blake and Mouton's Sales Grid 235
Learning Objectives 235
Introduction 235
Location 9,1 (Push-the-Product Orientation) 237
Location 1,9 (People Orientation) 238
Location 1,1 (Take-It-or-Leave-It Orientation) 238
Location 5,5 (Sales Routine Orientation) 238
Location 9,9 (Problem-Solving Orientation) 239
Operational Matters 239
Summary 241
Exercises 241
Reference 241

Preface

Marketing can broadly be defined as a management process that involves the assessment of customer wants and needs, and the performance of all activities associated with the development, pricing, provision, and promotion of product solutions that satisfy those wants and needs. Although most often associated with advertising and sales, marketing is much more encompassing, as its definition implies. Aside from promotions activities, marketing includes such critical functions as environmental scanning, wants and needs assessment, new product development, target marketing, product pricing, product distribution, and market research. Indeed, marketing is possibly the most critical management responsibility associated with the pursuit and realization of growth and prosperity.

While the discipline of marketing occupies a prominent position in virtually all for-profit institutions, its presence in nonprofit institutions is decidedly less pronounced; however, marketing is necessary for success, regardless of an institution's ownership, mission, or served markets. Although there is growing interest in exploiting the power of marketing in the nonprofit sector, its current and historic muted presence in this realm likely stems from the fact that the vast majority of marketing innovations were developed by scholars who had for-profit entities in mind when they designed and perfected given tools and techniques. As such, these developments typically found their way onto the pages of business textbooks and journals, rather than in nonprofit sector publications. Given this, these developments easily evaded the attention of academics, executives, and students focused on nonprofit administration.

Additionally, many of the current and historic marketing tools make use of language that, while commonplace in the for-profit sector, remains somewhat foreign in the nonprofit world. For example, many in the nonprofit sector might take offense that an admission to a medical clinic, a "hit" on a healthy lifestyles website, a phone call to a domestic abuse hotline, a book checked out at a community library, and a donation made to a blood bank all would constitute sales of some sort in the minds of business executives. To nonprofit executives who are not accustomed to the lingo, that perhaps might sound a bit harsh, but a sale indeed can constitute any form of desired exchange. The notion that a cash register must ring is simply inaccurate.

Indeed, the language barrier must be overcome if marketing is to ever flourish in the nonprofit world. Marketing tools will continue to be developed primarily by scholars based in business schools, so it will be imperative for those in the nonprofit sector who desire marketing success to take steps to cross over disciplinary lines, engage the literature of business administration, and adapt given innovations to their particular environments. Once this bridge is created, both in the academic and practitioner worlds of nonprofit administration, marketing will achieve a prominent place in nonprofit scholarship and daily organizational life. This particular text was authored in an effort to provide that very bridge.

Nonprofit Marketing presents a series of 35 essential marketing tools and demonstrates their application in the nonprofit sector, referencing myriad diverse entities, including zoological parks, planetariums, theater companies, medical clinics, workforce development centers, food banks, and more. The tools presented in this work cover a fairly broad spectrum of marketing, including product development and portfolio analysis; branding and identity management; target marketing; consumer behavior and product promotions; environmental analysis and competitive assessment; and marketing management, strategy, and planning.

While the specific tools selected from these broad categories are firmly entrenched in the for-profit world, the vast majority of them have never surfaced in the nonprofit sector. As noted earlier, to make sense of these tools, especially in some cases, a premium will be placed on the reader's ability to adapt to language that might be somewhat foreign in the nonprofit realm. Further, innovative thinking will be required to fully grasp the application potential of given tools. It also should be noted that, as there are myriad types of nonprofit entities, degree of applicability, in some cases, can vary considerably, depending on the particular type of nonprofit institution under examination.

Each chapter of this work focuses on a specific marketing tool and, if desired, can be read as a stand-alone document—a convenience that greatly increases the utility of *Nonprofit Marketing*. For additional assistance in gaining an understanding of marketing, especially for those with no exposure to the discipline, a brief introduction is offered in the appendix of this book. A glossary of marketing terminology is also included at the conclusion of this work.

It is my hope that you will find the tools and techniques presented in this book useful in your study of nonprofit marketing.

John L. Fortenberry, Jr.

PART I

Product Development and Portfolio Analysis Tools

CHAPTER 1

The Product Life Cycle

LEARNING OBJECTIVES

After examining this chapter, readers will have the ability to:

- Recognize that all product offerings possess limited life spans, necessitating appropriate product succession planning efforts.
- Appreciate the value of the Product Life Cycle as a tool for product succession planning and related product management activities, including portfolio planning, strategy formulation, and forecasting.
- Identify the four stages of the Product Life Cycle and understand methods for strategically and tactically managing offerings during each of these stages.
- Utilize the Product Life Cycle in the nonprofit sector to effect enhanced marketing outcomes.

INTRODUCTION

As with all living things, products, including those offered in the nonprofit sector, have finite life spans. There is no set life span, but in time all offerings will be replaced. Drivers of product obsolescence are numerous and vary depending on the nature of the given product offering. Technology certainly plays a role, as most any veteran librarian will well recall, having witnessed the decline of physical books, journals, and newspapers and the subsequent rise of electronic versions of the same. Imagine the community library that refused to adapt to the changing environment and revise its offerings accordingly.

Technological developments have affected colleges and universities as well, forcing them to realign their product portfolios to ensure survival, growth, and prosperity. Their age-old, core product offering of educational classes held in face-to-face settings is being challenged by classes offered in cyberspace, fueled by new online platforms that permit learning at a distance with virtually no encumbrances. Clearly, the modern age is taking some institutions out of their comfort zones, forcing them to enhance, upgrade, or produce altogether new offerings to please their target audiences.

Another common driver of product obsolescence is perhaps more finicky in that it simply pertains to changing customer preferences, desires, and expectations. A museum, for example, must be very cognizant of the fact that the latest, greatest exhibit likely will run its course and witness declining interest over time, necessitating an enhancement or replacement if patronage and financial support are to be retained. A public television or radio station, too, would need to ensure that it keeps its finger on the pulse of the consumer, as preferences can change quickly, which could potentially result in diminishing audiences and render the given nonprofit media company unviable.

Product obsolescence, regardless of its cause or particular time line, forces nonprofit executives to think about both today and tomorrow. They simply cannot afford to focus only on the current product offerings provided by their establishments. Instead, they also must actively seek to develop new products that will succeed those entering decline.

Not only do products possess limited life spans, but like their living counterparts, their life spans consist of a number of developmental stages, with each of these stages presenting its own unique array of opportunities and constraints. Indeed, products must be managed differently during the different stages of their life cycles, making it imperative for nonprofit executives to understand these stages and the appropriate strategies to be employed—a task facilitated by a model known as the Product Life Cycle. Illustrated in Figure 1-1, the Product Life Cycle consists of a vertical axis representing sales, a horizontal axis representing time, a curve illustrating sales growth in relation to time, and four stages of development: introduction, growth, maturity, and decline.

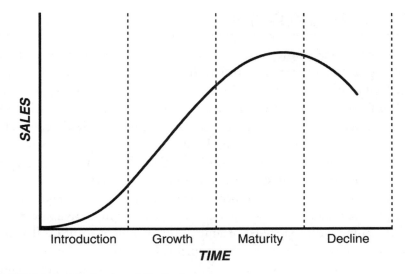

FIGURE 1-1 The Product Life Cycle

STAGE 1: INTRODUCTION

The introduction stage of the Product Life Cycle involves the initial presentation of a product in the market. During this stage, sales growth slowly begins to increase as the public gains awareness of newly introduced product offerings through promotional efforts. It is important to note that a "sale" would constitute any form of positive exchange (e.g., calls to a suicide prevention hotline, admissions at a charitable medical clinic, gate receipts at a zoo) depending on the nature of the nonprofit offering. Direct competitors in the market are few or nonexistent at this point. Here, nonprofit executives are primarily concerned with developing innovative promotional strategies that will increase product awareness in the market.

As an example, consider a suburban community that is experiencing rapid growth. The closest colleges are located miles away in the urban center of the region. A savvy college might decide to establish an outreach center in this burgeoning suburb for recruitment, classes, community events, and so on. Leading up to and following the grand opening of the outreach center, the college would do well to promote the importance of obtaining a college education, noting that it now can be obtained more conveniently than ever.

STAGE 2: GROWTH

The growth stage of the Product Life Cycle is characterized by rapidly escalating sales, courtesy of increased product awareness. This rapid sales growth generates significant, positive attention (e.g., cash inflow, publicity, community praise), but it also attracts competitors to the market who seek to gain similar benefits. This effect necessitates that organizations leverage garnered resources and ply them back into these products to fend off new entrants. During this stage, nonprofit executives shift their attention from building product awareness to building brand awareness. In other words, they direct efforts toward promoting their own, specific version of the noted product offering, providing defenses against competitive threats.

Continuing with the college example, the specific institution that initially established an outreach center in this burgeoning suburb can rest assured that if it experiences success, the competing colleges in the region will follow it into this particular market. Once these newcomers enter this suburban community, the first-in-market college must take steps to defend itself against these competitors, promoting its brand as being superior to others by providing the best educational choice for area citizens.

STAGE 3: MATURITY

During the maturity stage of the Product Life Cycle, sales growth levels off in what has now become an established market. Plateauing sales growth causes weaker competitors to exit the market, leaving their stronger counterparts to compete for market dominance. At this point, products are the most lucrative for their organizations. Because mature offerings are established in the market, it is not necessary to reinvest the entirety of resources that these products generate. Here, nonprofit executives seek to increase market share by further differentiating their products from competitive offerings.

Further extending the college example, as a mature market, this suburban community now features multiple colleges competing for students and other patrons. This once open market is now saturated. Competition reaches its fever pitch and, over time, the strong will emerge and dominate; the weak will retreat or hold diminished positions. Here, overt efforts must be taken to communicate to the public why degree offerings from College A are superior to those offered by Colleges B, C, and D.

Perhaps College A can tout that it possesses a higher level of accreditation, better value, more degree offerings, or some other unique feature that can be used to convince residents to look to it, rather than competitors, for educational wants and needs.

STAGE 4: DECLINE

During the decline stage of the Product Life Cycle, sales growth rapidly decreases, as does the number of competitors in the marketplace. Falling consumer demand leads establishments to either eliminate these products or seek to extend the life spans of declining offerings through the discovery of new product uses or through product repositioning.

Wrapping up the college example, if the given suburb reaches its peak and the population shifts back to the central urban area or perhaps to a new suburban area, the college's outreach center would likely find itself with a smaller pool of potential prospects and witness declining enrollments. In such cases, the college might seek to withdraw from the community if the decline is severe enough. Alternatively, it could seek to alter its scope and mission in the community. If it had focused solely on graduate offerings, for example, perhaps it could add undergraduate offerings, or possibly even vocational and technical training, to its product mix in hopes of stemming declines.

PRODUCT LIFE CYCLE VARIANTS

Although typically illustrated as an S-shaped curve, the appearance of the Product Life Cycle varies based on the marketplace experiences of product offerings. Figure 1-2 illustrates six curves that could potentially develop.

Figure 1-2A illustrates the life cycle of a product that witnessed a very lengthy ascent to maturity. This lengthy ascent possibly occurred because the public was not ready or willing to accept the new offering or perhaps because the entity had difficulties informing the public of the new product's existence. Any newly established nonprofit entity seeking to enter established markets with established competitors would likely face this type of life cycle scenario as it strives to develop a clientele base.

Figure 1-2B depicts the life cycle of a product that gained immediate acceptance followed by a period of enduring maturity. Such a curve would possibly develop upon the placement of a charitable medical clinic in

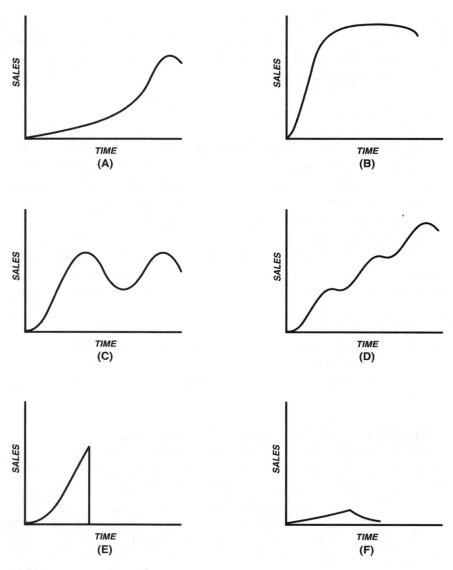

FIGURE 1-2 Product Life Cycle Variants

a rural community previously unaddressed by medical practitioners. Such an endeavor would be immediately welcomed by residents, resulting in a better-served community, steadfast patronage for the clinic, and mission fulfillment.

Figure 1-2C depicts the life cycle of a product that entered maturity, declined, reentered maturity, and reentered decline. This cyclical pattern would be representative of, for example, a veterans support organization that experiences the ebb and flow of need from servicemen and servicewomen in tandem with transitions between peacetime and wartime.

Figure 1-2D illustrates the life cycle of a product that reentered the growth stage multiple times after reaching maturity. An example of such a product would be a zoological park that routinely, at the first sign of decline, took steps to bolster its exhibits and offerings, which generated new interest and attention, resulting in extended growth beyond its initial maturity stage.

Figure 1-2E illustrates the life cycle of a product that experienced a period of rapid growth followed by an immediate decline. This type of curve would be representative of, for example, a blood bank that was suddenly shut down due to safety violations. This curve would also be illustrative of a homeless shelter that was forced to close because of reduced support by volunteers and financial contributors.

Figure 1-2F illustrates the life cycle of a product that failed after its introduction into the market. This unfortunate life cycle could represent any of the multiple new nonprofit initiatives that are introduced into the market but fail to achieve commercial success.

These examples illustrate only a few of the many Product Life Cycle variants that could possibly develop. Obviously, there are no guarantees that products will move through any or all of the stages of development. Given the unpredictable nature of product and market dynamics, it stands to reason that Product Life Cycles cannot be predetermined.

OPERATIONAL MATTERS

Given that all products have limited lives, nonprofit executives must actively assemble and manage product portfolios that are formulated to achieve long-term growth and prosperity. The Product Life Cycle assists nonprofit executives in this endeavor, serving as a useful portfolio-planning tool. Ideally, organizations will have products at all stages of the Product Life Cycle. By assembling balanced product portfolios, nonprofit executives position their organizations for consistent, enduring growth.

In addition to its strength as a portfolio-planning tool, the Product Life Cycle also serves as a guide for designing marketing strategies.

Because different developmental stages require different marketing actions, the Product Life Cycle provides nonprofit executives with a decision-making tool for formulating marketing strategy.

The Product Life Cycle can also be used as a forecasting tool where efforts are made to predict the Product Life Cycles of new and anticipated product offerings (Levitt, 1965). Even though Product Life Cycles cannot be predetermined, marketing strategy can be improved by formulating potential life cycle scenarios.

SUMMARY

The Product Life Cycle provides nonprofit executives with an effective tool for portfolio planning, strategy formulation, and forecasting. It serves as a reminder of the limited life spans possessed by products and hence the necessity for product succession planning—an essential marketing task in an ever-changing world. The insights offered by the Product Life Cycle can greatly improve the marketing performance of nonprofit organizations.

EXERCISES

1. Define and comprehensively discuss the Product Life Cycle and its four associated stages, providing an illustration of this important marketing tool. Direct appropriate attention to the Product Life Cycle's use in portfolio planning, strategy formulation, and forecasting. Share your thoughts regarding the tool's implications and uses in the nonprofit sector.

2. Contact a local nonprofit entity and arrange an informational interview with its top executive. Present the Product Life Cycle and request insights regarding the appearance of the particular curves for several of the entity's product offerings. Does the given nonprofit entity actively use the Product Life Cycle as a tool for portfolio planning, strategy formulation, and forecasting? What other tools does the organization employ for such endeavors? Report your findings in detail.

REFERENCE

Levitt, T. (1965, November/December). Exploit the product life cycle. *Harvard Business Review, 43,* 81–94.

CHAPTER 2

Booz, Allen, and Hamilton's New Product Process

LEARNING OBJECTIVES

After examining this chapter, readers will have the ability to:

- Recognize the importance of nonprofit entities engaging in new product development as a means of ensuring enduring growth and prosperity.
- Understand associated barriers to new product development that complicate such initiatives.
- Appreciate the value provided by Booz, Allen, and Hamilton's New Product Process, guiding new product development activities from strategy development and idea generation through commercialization.

INTRODUCTION

Given that all products possess limited life spans, nonprofit executives must continually seek to develop new product offerings that will ensure long-term growth and prosperity. These new products, of course, do not automatically appear in the marketplace. Instead, they result from labor intensive, expensive, and bureaucratic efforts that eventually lead to market entry. Operating plans must be devised; logos must be designed and developed; corporations must be formed; building and operating permits must be acquired; property, plant, and equipment must be obtained; and so on, with each of these activities having associated costs. Even if market entry is attained, there are no guarantees of success, as indicated by the high incidence of new product failure.

In addition to the effort, expense, and bureaucracy associated with new product development, nonprofit entities face yet another concern. Every time new products are introduced to the market, these organizations place their reputations in jeopardy. New products that are poorly developed can be quite damaging to existing offerings, providing an additional incentive for nonprofit organizations to work diligently to ensure new product success.

MINIMIZING RISK

Although risk is inherent in new product development, it can be lessened by adopting a systematic framework for managing new product activities. One such framework for managing new product activities was developed by the management consulting firm of Booz, Allen, and Hamilton (currently known as Booz & Company). Illustrated in Figure 2-1, Booz, Allen, and Hamilton's New Product Process divides new product development into seven sequential stages: new product strategy development,

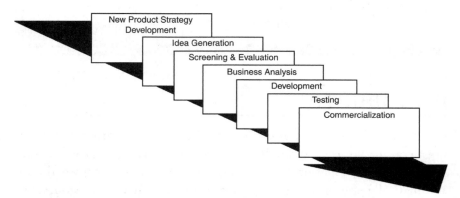

From New Products Management for the 1980s by Booz & Company. Copyright © 1982 by Booz & Company. Reprinted by permission of Booz & Company.

FIGURE 2-1 Booz, Allen, and Hamilton's New Product Process

idea generation, screening and evaluation, business analysis, development, testing, and commercialization. These stages are explained as follows.

STAGE 1: NEW PRODUCT STRATEGY DEVELOPMENT

Booz, Allen, and Hamilton's New Product Process begins with the development of new product strategies. Here, nonprofit executives lay the foundation for the new product process by reviewing missions and associated objectives, identifying roles that new products might play in satisfying given directives. This information clarifies the strategic requirements for new products and provides a point of reference for subsequent new product development stages.

STAGE 2: IDEA GENERATION

During the idea generation stage, nonprofit executives search for product ideas that are compatible with the goals and objectives determined in the preceding stage. The idea generation stage usually begins by conducting a self-assessment to determine the product categories that are of primary interest. When areas of interest have been determined, nonprofit executives scan the environment in search of growth opportunities. Ideas should actively be solicited from any potential idea source, including employees, customers, and vendors. The ultimate purpose of the idea generation stage is to produce a wealth of ideas. Every idea should be welcomed and initially considered on a "can do" basis.

STAGE 3: SCREENING AND EVALUATION

The screening and evaluation stage involves the analysis all the ideas gathered during the idea generation stage to determine which discoveries should be further investigated. Here, each idea should be envisioned as a product in the market where it can be evaluated on its potential contribution to given entities. Through screening and evaluation, nonprofit executives seek to narrow down the number of ideas generated during the preceding stage by focusing only on those that offer the greatest potential.

During this stage, new product ideas decrease; however, the expenses associated with new product development increase—a trend that

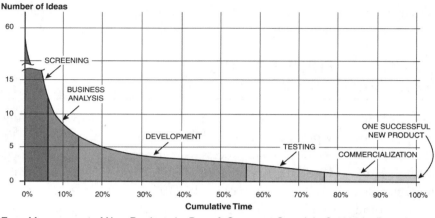

From Management of New Products by Booz & Company. Copyright © 1968 by Booz & Company. Reprinted by permission of Booz & Company.

FIGURE 2-2 Mortality of New Product Ideas

continues through the remaining stages of the new product process, as indicated in Figures 2-2 and 2-3, respectively. Organizations can only afford to develop those ideas that possess the greatest potential for success in the market. The most promising ideas proceed to the business analysis stage, and all others are eliminated.

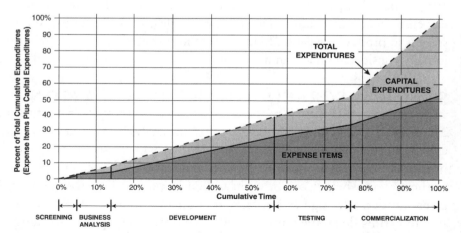

From Management of New Products by Booz & Company. Copyright © 1968 by Booz & Company. Reprinted by permission of Booz & Company.

FIGURE 2-3 Cumulative New Product Expenditures

STAGE 4: BUSINESS ANALYSIS

During the business analysis stage, the most promising product ideas are subjected to intense scrutiny to determine their potential for translation into viable offerings. Hypothetical business plans that identify product attributes, barriers to entry, current and potential competitors, target markets, market growth information, financial projections, promotional methods, and so on are created for these offerings in an effort to formulate preliminary recommendations. Successful product ideas graduate to the development stage.

STAGE 5: DEVELOPMENT

During the development stage, product ideas that have successfully met the scrutiny forwarded during prior stages are translated into actual product offerings. For goods, development involves the actual physical assembly of the offerings. For services, development involves the assembly of all components required for the services to be offered, such as office space, equipment, operating permits, and personnel. During this stage, product offerings may go through many alterations—a common occurrence when on-paper ideas are translated into real-world offerings. Alterations continue through the remaining stages of the new product process as goods and services are readied for the market.

STAGE 6: TESTING

Testing seeks to validate earlier projections associated with new offerings through experimentation. Here, new products are readied for market entry by conducting trials to determine marketplace suitability, with the nature of the testing being dependent on the characteristics of the particular products under development and the markets sought.

Because of their tangibility, goods are particularly well suited for laboratory testing and test marketing—a practice where nonprofit executives directly or indirectly seek consumer feedback regarding their new products. For example, an antismoking foundation preparing a comic book targeting the youth that emphasizes the need to abstain from the use of cigarettes and other tobacco products would subject this product to intensive testing to ensure that it communicates the desired messages effectively. Counselors, antismoking advocates, educators, researchers, and graphic artists would be consulted to ensure message content and effectiveness. This foundation would also be likely to test market this publication, permitting both parents and their children to read review copies of the comic book prior to its market-wide release in exchange for their feedback.

Like their tangible counterparts, services can also be tested and test marketed, albeit in a different manner. Certainly, prior to its grand opening, a planetarium would undergo an intensive battery of tests to ensure that equipment is working properly, that necessary supplies are available, that employees understand their duties and responsibilities, and so on. The planetarium might even decide to engage in test marketing by inviting a group of consumers to visit the establishment, view a particular show, and provide feedback on the experience.

The feedback generated through testing provides nonprofit executives with yet another opportunity to ready their products for entry into the marketplace. After any necessary alterations have been made, products are ready for commercialization.

STAGE 7: COMMERCIALIZATION

Commercialization involves the full-scale market introduction of newly developed products. As new products enter the market, ongoing customer feedback should actively be sought to ensure that products meet and, ideally, exceed customer expectations. Any new product "bugs" that are identified should quickly be remedied. Aside from ensuring a trouble-free marketplace introduction, nonprofit executives must carefully monitor competitor reactions to their new product offerings, taking steps when necessary to counteract competitive responses.

RISK AND FAILURE

Risk is an inherent part of new product development where new product failures routinely outnumber successes. Indeed, new product difficulties are prevalent across all industries and sectors. These failures are caused by a variety of factors, as illustrated in Table 2-1.

Despite these risks, nonprofit entities must engage in the new product process if they wish to endure and prosper. Only through the adoption of a systematic framework for managing new product activities can nonprofit

Table 2-1 Causes of New Product Failure

1. **Market/marketing failure**
    - Small size of the potential market
    - No clear product differentiation
    - Poor positioning
    - Misunderstanding of customer needs
    - Lack of channel support
    - Competitive response
2. **Financial failure**
    - Low return on investment
3. **Timing failure**
    - Late in the market
    - Too early—market not yet developed
4. **Technical failure**
    - Product did not work
    - Bad design
5. **Organizational failure**
    - Poor fit with the organizational culture
    - Lack of organizational support
6. **Environmental failure**
    - Government regulations
    - Macroeconomic factors

Source: From Jain, D. (2001). Managing new product development for strategic competitive advantage. In D. Iacobucci (Ed.), *Kellogg on marketing* (pp. 130–150). New York, NY: Wiley. Copyright © 2001 by John Wiley & Sons, Inc. Reprinted with permission of John Wiley & Sons, Inc.

executives minimize associated risks and increase their chances of developing new goods and services that achieve success in the marketplace.

SUMMARY

Booz, Allen, and Hamilton's New Product Process serves as a useful guide for new product development. Its seven sequential stages—new product strategy development, idea generation, screening and evaluation, business analysis, development, testing, and commercialization—provide invaluable guidance to nonprofit executives seeking to develop new products in a comprehensive and orderly fashion.

EXERCISES

1. Provide a detailed account profiling Booz, Allen, and Hamilton's New Product Process, identifying and explaining each of its seven steps, accompanied by an appropriate illustration. Discuss the rigors of new product development as they impact the nonprofit sector. Share your thoughts on the degree to which modern nonprofit organizations follow a systematic new product development process, such as that offered by Booz, Allen, and Hamilton.

2. Contact a local nonprofit entity and arrange an informational interview with its top executive to learn about the organization's new product development practices. Specifically request information about the trials and tribulations associated with any recent or historic product launches. Present Booz, Allen, and Hamilton's New Product Process to this executive and ask about the degree to which his or her organization follows such a process. Report your findings in detail.

REFERENCES

Booz, Allen, & Hamilton. (1968). *Management of new products*. New York, NY: Author.

Booz, Allen, & Hamilton. (1982). *New products management for the 1980s*. New York, NY: Author.

Jain, D. (2001). Managing new product development for strategic competitive advantage. In D. Iacobucci (Ed.), *Kellogg on marketing* (pp. 130–150). New York, NY: Wiley.

CHAPTER 3

George Day's R-W-W Screen

LEARNING OBJECTIVES

After examining this chapter, readers will have the ability to:

- Understand that new product development in the nonprofit sector involves the assumption of risk but also offers the potential for reward.
- Realize that the constantly changing marketplace mandates that nonprofit executives engage in new product development to increase the likelihood of survival, growth, and prosperity.
- Recognize that, as new product development represents a mandatory pursuit, reduction of risk becomes the prevailing consideration.
- Appreciate George Day's R-W-W Screen as a tool for reducing the risk associated with new product development, increasing the likelihood of successful new product endeavors.

INTRODUCTION

New product development in the nonprofit sector is a process teeming with both risk and reward. The risk is associated with the large investments of time and money required to launch new offerings. Additionally, nonprofit organizations place their reputations on the line when fielding new products.

The risks associated with new product development certainly represent a deterrent to engagement in this process, but only through the development and launch of new and improved offerings can nonprofit entities position themselves for enduring marketplace success, yielding the associated rewards. Thus, new product development should be viewed as a mandatory pursuit. Reduction of risk becomes the prevailing consideration.

While there are no guarantees that new products will be successful, there are techniques that can be employed to reduce associated risk and increase the likelihood of success. One such technique, offered by George Day, is known as the R-W-W Screen. Presented in Figure 3-1, Day's

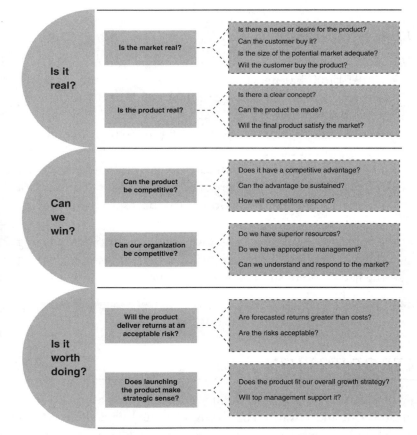

FIGURE 3-1 George Day's R-W-W Screen

R-W-W Screen essentially consists of three primary questions, each containing an array of more specific questions that are to be addressed in any new product venture. The R-W-W descriptor is derived from the first letter of key words in the set of primary questions: (1) Is it <u>R</u>eal? (2) Can we <u>W</u>in? and (3) Is it <u>W</u>orth doing? These three questions and associated inquiries are explained as follows.

IS IT REAL?

The "Is it real?" inquiry pertains to market and product viability, calling on nonprofit executives to answer two second-level questions ("Is the market real?" and "Is the product real?") and a series of related inquiries flowing from each.

Nonprofit executives must assess whether the market is of adequate size, whether targeted customers want or need the offering, and whether the customers have the means (independently or through associated funding parties) and desire to purchase the product. For example, a symphony orchestra in a smaller city might indeed fill a marketplace want or need, and citizens may very well have the means and desire to forward their patronage, but the population may simply be too small to support such an offering. Of course, there are circumstances where populations in smaller cities might be capable of supporting a symphony orchestra. Only through prudent market research can such determinations be made.

As for the product, assessments must determine if the given offering is well conceptualized, can actually be produced, and is capable of satisfying customers. A church venturing into, say, the provision of a day care center for the children of members is faced with myriad decisions associated with such an offering. Trained personnel must be acquired, along with special-ized learning resources and other equipment. A proper facility, appropriate furnishings and fixtures, and, of course, the permission of regulatory bodies must be obtained. Even if the provision of a child day care center is feasible, one still must investigate whether the offering will be capable of meeting and, ideally, exceeding customer wants and needs.

CAN WE WIN?

The "Can we win?" inquiry pertains to product and institutional competitiveness, calling on nonprofit executives to answer two second-tier questions ("Can the product be competitive?" and "Can our organization be competitive?") and associated inquiries. Nonprofit executives should not be dismayed by the term *competition* and its variants, all firmly entrenched in the language of the for-profit world. Instead, those operating in the nonprofit sector must realize that their organizations also exist in a competitive world, with their offerings competing against others directly or indirectly.

As for product competitiveness, assessments must ascertain whether new offerings have a sustainable competitive advantage over other offerings and what, if any, response will be forwarded by competitors with the launch of the potential new offering. For example, a private day school seeking to enter a given marketplace without a competitive advantage will struggle for market share. Even if the offering has an initial edge, if it is not sustainable, any gains generated will be lost to more savvy rivals. Therefore, it is imperative to ensure that offerings incorporate a sustainable competitive advantage that will distinguish them from current and potential offerings.

The private day school's competitive advantage might be that it incorporates Christian teachings in its curriculum and associated activities, something that clearly would distinguish it from public school offerings in the area. Of course, regardless of advantage, competitive responses to new offerings must be envisioned. Perhaps the private day school will witness the establishment of another in the marketplace, copying its points of differentiation and posing a threat to market share and associated prosperity. For this reason, nonprofit executives must always be thinking about how their product offerings can be advanced further by incorporating new sources of competitive advantage to stay ahead of the competition.

As for organizational competitiveness, nonprofit executives must investigate the availability of resources and presence of qualified personnel. Behind every product stands the organization that produces and provides the offering. A poorly resourced entity is sure to encounter difficulties even if its new product development efforts yield a successful launch, as those competitors who possess superior resources will have the upper hand. Of course, nonprofit executives must be astute observers of the marketplace, being ready, willing, and able to act on any potential opportunity.

IS IT WORTH DOING?

The "Is it worth doing?" inquiry pertains to risk/return and strategic appropriateness, calling on nonprofit executives to answer two second-tier questions ("Will the product deliver returns at an acceptable risk?" and "Does launching the product make strategic sense?") and a series of related inquiries.

As for risk/return, nonprofit executives must determine if returns will be greater than costs and whether risks are acceptable. Quite obviously, there are situations in the nonprofit sector where entities are compelled to offer services that do not generate any sort of financial return from the service recipients themselves, yet the provision of associated services is necessary to fulfill given missions. In such cases, considerations must include the presence (or absence) of third-party generosity in associated return formulas, further demonstrating that nonprofit executives must understand their products, clients served, stakeholders, and financial supporters. Of course, risk is ever present in new product development, but such risk must not exceed a tolerable level.

As for strategic appropriateness, assessments must determine if products are suited for the overall strategy of given nonprofit organizations and whether top executives and other contributors will offer support. New offerings must be viewed in the context of the existing offerings and must make sense as new additions within associated product portfolios. They, too, must be championed by top-level nonprofit executives and key financial supporters because new product pursuits require ongoing attention and resources that only these parties can provide.

OPERATIONAL MATTERS

Implementation of Day's R-W-W Screen simply involves asking each of the questions indicated in Figure 3-1 and answering the inquiries intelligently and honestly. Clearly, the instance of any definite "no" answer for questions in the first and second columns of the diagram is grounds for immediate termination of the idea, and the instance of a definite "no" answer in third-column inquiries strongly signals that development should not be pursued.

Because the information needed to address the inquiries identified in Day's R-W-W Screen is intensive and the impact of new products affects multiple units within nonprofit organizations, it is advised that interdisciplinary teams be created to assess each inquiry. Such teams must endeavor to avoid viewing the instrument as an obstacle to overcome, something that can occur when team members are especially passionate about new product ideas, and look for ways to circumvent barriers that suggest idea termination. It is absolutely imperative that inquiries identified in Day's R-W-W Screen be addressed in a completely objective fashion.

It is important to realize that Day's R-W-W Screen should be used on multiple occasions throughout the stages of product development. This repetition is essential because initial conceptions of products often change as they work their way through the various developmental processes, sometimes emerging as manifestations far removed from initial designs. Deployment of Day's R-W-W Screen across the multiple stages of product development ensures that new product efforts remain worthwhile.

SUMMARY

George Day's R-W-W Screen provides much needed guidance to nonprofit executives in their endeavors to determine the viability of new product ideas. Importantly, this tool can be utilized to minimize the risk associated with new product development, increasing the likelihood that new goods and services will launch productively and successfully.

EXERCISES

1. Provide a detailed account profiling George Day's R-W-W Screen, identifying and explaining its components, purposes, methods of implementation, and practical applications, accompanied by an appropriate illustration. Preface your discussion by offering an overview of the risk and return associated with new product development in the nonprofit sector. Share your thoughts regarding the tool's implications and uses in nonprofit organizations.

2. Conduct a review of journals, websites, and other sources in an effort to identify articles that describe various nonprofit product missteps. From these accounts, identify and describe the mistakes that led to failure. Could the use of George Day's R-W-W Screen have prevented these mistakes/failures? If so, how?

REFERENCE

Day, G. S. (2007, December). Is it real? Can we win? Is it worth doing? Managing risk and reward in an innovation portfolio. *Harvard Business Review*, *85*, 110–120.

CHAPTER 4

Theodore Levitt's Total Product Concept

LEARNING OBJECTIVES

After examining this chapter, readers will have the ability to:

- Recognize that products consist of multiple levels of attributes, ideally assembled in such a manner as to meet and exceed the expectations of target audiences.
- Understand that product attributes must continually be enhanced and improved to maintain relevance in the lives of target audiences.
- Realize the value of Theodore Levitt's Total Product Concept as an aid in developing these multiple levels of attributes to increase the likelihood that associated offerings will continually meet and exceed customer wants and needs.

INTRODUCTION

Products are much more than one-dimensional items. Instead, they represent complex bundles of attributes meant to satisfy customers' wants and needs. The success of goods and services in the marketplace is largely based on the skillful assembly of associated product attributes in a manner that will meet and exceed customer expectations. Therefore, nonprofit executives must possess a thorough understanding of the multidimensional nature of products.

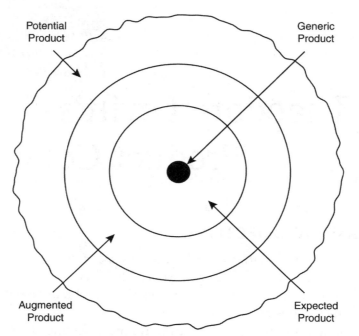

FIGURE 4-1 Levitt's Total Product Concept

The Total Product Concept, formulated by Theodore Levitt, illustrates the multidimensional nature of products and provides guidance to nonprofit executives seeking to develop goods and services that fully address customer wants and needs. Presented in Figure 4-1, Levitt's Total Product Concept depicts four product levels—generic, expected, augmented, and potential— which are illustrated by four concentric circles. As products move from inner levels to outer levels, they become increasingly complex and offer enhanced opportunities to differentiate them from competitive offerings.

THE GENERIC PRODUCT

The generic product, which could also be referred to as the core product, is an offering in its most basic and rudimentary form. At this level, competitive products are virtually indistinguishable from one another as they represent only core offerings and nothing more. Customers expect more than these basic offerings.

THE EXPECTED PRODUCT

The expected product consists of the generic product along with features that allow it to be distinguished from competitive offerings. Expected products add branding, product features, product quality, packaging, and like elements to generic products to create offerings that are easily recognized by customers. At this level, goods and services meet the minimum expectations of customers. In essence, these offerings represent what customers *expect* to receive.

THE AUGMENTED PRODUCT

The augmented product consists of the expected product plus additional features that extend beyond the expectations of customers. Product augmentations vary based on the nature of the given offerings, but typical examples include personalized service, warranties and guarantees, extended service plans, and financial assistance. Augmentations allow nonprofit executives to further differentiate their products from competitive offerings. The differentiation offered by specific augmentations may decline over time as consumers become accustomed to the enhancements and come to expect these additions, necessitating that nonprofit executives discover new ways to augment their products.

THE POTENTIAL PRODUCT

The potential product represents all things that may potentially be incorporated into offerings to attract and retain customers. Whereas augmented products represent everything that is *currently* being done to attract and retain customers, potential products represent everything that *might* be done. As current augmentations become expected by customers, nonprofit executives must formulate future methods to augment, and thus differentiate, their products. The potential product level identifies these future augmentations.

OPERATIONAL MATTERS

To assess products using Levitt's Total Product Concept, nonprofit executives simply (1) identify the product to be evaluated, (2) construct the Total Product Concept diagram, as illustrated in Figure 4-1, (3) identify and/or formulate the generic, expected, augmented, and potential components for the product under evaluation, and (4) place the identified components on the diagram accordingly. The resulting Total Product Concept diagram is then analyzed to gain product insights.

Figure 4-2 provides an example of Levitt's Total Product Concept applied to a botanical garden. The core offering provided by the garden would be an educational, entertaining experience, courtesy of its various exhibits. This generic offering is transformed into an expected product

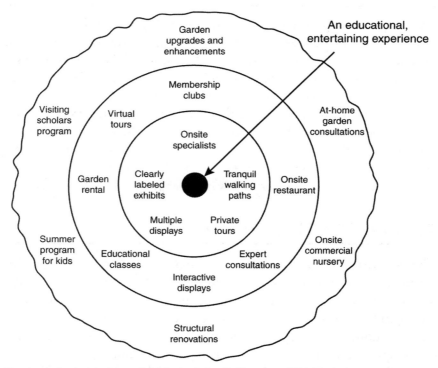

Constructed using design methodologies in Levitt, Theodore. 1980. Marketing success through differentiation—of anything. *Harvard Business Review* (January–February): 83–91.

FIGURE 4-2 A Botanical Garden's Total Product Concept

through a variety of additions, including tranquil walking paths, highly varied display gardens, clearly labeled exhibits, private tours for individuals and groups, and onsite specialists available to provide further information. The botanical garden hopes to further differentiate itself from its competitors (both direct and indirect) through a series of augmentations; namely, opportunities to rent the garden for special events, an onsite restaurant, educational classes, interactive learning technologies, and related enhancements. Future differentiation could occur through renovations, at-home garden consultations, an onsite commercial nursery, and so on.

Figure 4-3 provides an example of Levitt's Total Product Concept applied to an assisted living center. The center's generic product consists of

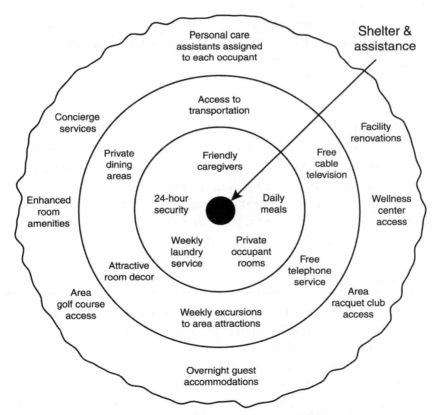

Constructed using design methodologies in Levitt, Theodore. 1980. Marketing success through differentiation—of anything. *Harvard Business Review* (January–February): 83–91.

FIGURE 4-3 An Assisted Living Center's Total Product Concept

the shelter and assistance that it offers to occupants. This base offering is transformed into the expected product through various features, including private occupant rooms, round-the-clock security, daily meals, weekly laundry service, and related amenities. Augmentations include weekly excursions to area attractions, access to transportation, private dining facilities, and so on. Future differentiation opportunities exist through overnight accommodations for guests, enhanced room amenities, personal care assistants assigned to each occupant, and related product upgrades.

Clearly, Levitt's Total Product Concept reminds nonprofit executives that products represent complex bundles of attributes that must skillfully be assembled to satisfy customers. It also serves as an excellent product planning and analysis tool for the level-by-level dissection of current and proposed products. Through this dissection, nonprofit executives can identify and, if necessary, enhance those attributes that differentiate products from competitive offerings. They also can formulate strategies for the future differentiation of goods and services. These points of differentiation are especially useful in the development of effective promotional campaigns.

SUMMARY

Levitt's Total Product Concept clearly illustrates the multidimensional nature of products. By understanding the product levels identified in the Total Product Concept, nonprofit executives are better prepared to assemble the multiple attributes of goods and services in a manner that will attract and retain customers.

EXERCISES

1. Provide a comprehensive overview of Theodore Levitt's Total Product Concept, explaining its purpose, components, uses, and benefits, accompanied by an associated illustration. Be sure to indicate how the model focuses not only on current product manifestations but also on future perspectives of product offerings. Share your views regarding how this instrument can be used to effect better product management outcomes in the nonprofit sector.

2. Place yourself in the position of a nonprofit entrepreneur seeking to investigate opportunities for a new product offering of your choice in your local market. Using Theodore Levitt's Total Product Concept, develop an associated diagram for the given offering, identifying attributes pertaining to each level indicated in the model. Provide a narrative to accompany this diagram, discussing your thought process for assembling the product in the manner illustrated.

REFERENCES

Levitt, T. (1980, January/February). Marketing success through differentiation—of anything. *Harvard Business Review, 58*, 83–91.

Levitt, T. (1986). *The marketing imagination* (Exp. ed.). New York, NY: The Free Press.

The Boston Consulting Group's Growth/Share Matrix

LEARNING OBJECTIVES

After examining this chapter, readers will have the ability to:
- Understand the importance of assembling balanced product portfolios as a means of ensuring extended success in the marketplace.
- Realize the value of the Boston Consulting Group's Growth/ Share Matrix as a device for assessing the product portfolios of nonprofit entities.
- Effect prudent product management decisions on the basis of the growth and market share characteristics of given goods and services, as determined by the positioning of such offerings in the Boston Consulting Group's Growth/Share Matrix.

INTRODUCTION

Successful nonprofit organizations must strive to assemble balanced product portfolios that will ensure lasting success in the marketplace. Because all products have defined life spans, it is necessary to plan for the future by developing new products that will eventually succeed mature offerings.

The successful assembly of a balanced product portfolio requires that nonprofit executives maintain a keen awareness of the characteristics of the products they are responsible for managing. This awareness is attained, in part, by conducting a portfolio analysis. Through such an analysis, nonprofit executives comprehensively review their product offerings in an effort to identify strengths and weaknesses, making alterations and enhancements as necessary.

To analyze product portfolios, nonprofit executives often rely on the Boston Consulting Group's Growth/Share Matrix. Illustrated in Figure 5-1, the Growth/Share Matrix assesses products based on market growth and market share characteristics.

Market growth is a measure of a market's momentum or lack thereof, while market share is a measure of an entity's portion of the total sales generated by a given product in a given market. It is important to remember that a "sale" may constitute any form of desired exchange (e.g., calls to a runaway hotline, admissions at a drug and alcohol rehabilitation center,

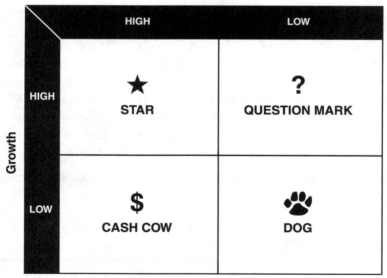

FIGURE 5-1 The Boston Consulting Group's Growth/Share Matrix

gate receipts at a planetarium) depending on the nature of the nonprofit offering. The Growth/Share Matrix consists of a vertical axis representing market growth (high and low), a horizontal axis representing market share (high and low), and four cells identified as cash cows, stars, question marks, and dogs. These four cells are explained as follows.

CASH COWS (LOW GROWTH, HIGH MARKET SHARE)

A cash cow is a product that possesses a strong market position in a low-growth market. Cash cows generate large amounts of cash (received directly from the product recipients themselves or indirectly through third-party payers), typically in excess of the amount required to maintain the given offering. Hence, the sizeable revenues that they generate can be used to develop other goods and services in associated portfolios.

STARS (HIGH GROWTH, HIGH MARKET SHARE)

A star is a product that possesses a significant share of a rapidly growing market. Although stars generate large amounts of cash, the cash must be reinvested in the given products to maintain market share in their high-growth environments. If stars maintain their market positions, they will eventually become cash cows when market growth levels off along with the associated reinvestment requirements.

QUESTION MARKS (HIGH GROWTH, LOW MARKET SHARE)

A question mark is a product that has a weak market position in an environment of rapid growth. Although the market is quite attractive, the market share possessed by these product offerings is not. If question marks maintain their market positions, they will eventually become dogs. However, if market share can be increased, question marks can become stars and eventually cash cows. Increasing market share, however, requires significant investment, which must come from other sources because question marks cannot independently generate the necessary cash.

DOGS (LOW GROWTH, LOW MARKET SHARE)

A dog is a product that possesses a weak market position in an environment of little growth. Dogs are generally cash drains on entities, and even when they do show positive returns, these funds must be reinvested to maintain market share. Unless compensating factors exist, dogs should ideally be divested, freeing resources to be directed toward more prosperous pursuits.

MARKET DYNAMICS

Because market growth eventually slows down, all products will eventually become either cash cows or dogs. This fact necessitates that nonprofit executives diligently pursue market leadership positions for all of their products during periods of growth. Leadership positions will pay dividends when growth slows and reinvestment requirements become minimal.

OPERATIONAL MATTERS

To assess products using the Boston Consulting Group's Growth/Share Matrix, nonprofit executives must simply (1) identify the offerings they wish to assess, (2) construct the Growth/Share Matrix, as illustrated in Figure 5-1, (3) gather product-related growth/share data, and (4) plot each product on the Growth/Share Matrix using circles, with larger circles representing products with larger shares of the market than smaller circles represent.

This visual representation is then analyzed to determine the strengths and weaknesses associated with given product portfolios. If additional detail is desired, nonprofit executives can forecast the market positions of products at some point in the future and plot these predictions on the Growth/Share Matrix using contrasting circles.

Figure 5-2 identifies a Growth/Share Matrix (current and forecasted) that was developed for a rural medical center. The eight white circles identify the medical center's eight product offerings designated by departmental unit. These units include the medical center's nursing home, surgery department, emergency department, occupational health clinic, assisted living center, home health agency, primary care clinic,

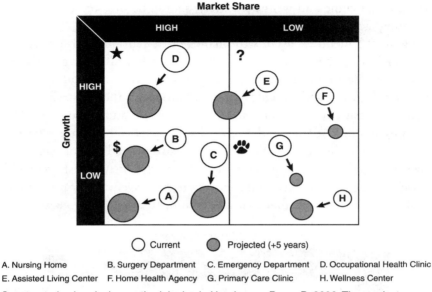

○ Current   ● Projected (+5 years)

A. Nursing Home   B. Surgery Department   C. Emergency Department   D. Occupational Health Clinic
E. Assisted Living Center   F. Home Health Agency   G. Primary Care Clinic   H. Wellness Center

Constructed using design methodologies in Henderson, Bruce D. 2006. The product portfolio (1970). In the Boston Consulting Group on strategy: Classic concepts and new perspectives, 2nd ed., ed. Carl W. Stern and Michael S. Deimler. New York: Wiley.

FIGURE 5-2 A Rural Medical Center's Growth/Share Matrix

and wellness center. The eight shaded circles represent the market share estimates for these products in five years. A review of this diagram indicates that the medical center currently has three cash cows, one star, two question marks, and two dogs.

Overall, the current and forecasted portfolios of this facility appear to be very strong. The medical center is fortunate to have three cash cows generating revenues that can be used to fund other product offerings. With continued investment, its star can be converted into a cash cow as its market matures. The question marks must be evaluated carefully to determine each unit's potential contribution. If the five-year forecast is accurate, it appears that the assisted living center represents a worthwhile investment because it is anticipated to become a star. However, the home health agency is expected to lose market share and drift into the dog quadrant. The home health agency, along with the two dogs (i.e., the primary care clinic and wellness center), should be divested unless compensating factors exist.

Figure 5-3 identifies a Growth/Share Matrix (current and forecasted) that was developed for a thrift shop with stores in five different geographic locations: Washington County, Adams County, Jefferson County, Madison County, and Lincoln County. Currently, the thrift shop possesses one cash cow, one star, no question marks, and three dogs. The Washington and Adams markets are clearly beneficial and are expected to remain so in the future. The Jefferson, Madison, and Lincoln markets, however, represent portfolio liabilities. Obviously, the thrift shop would do well to exit these markets and concentrate exclusively on the prosperous Washington and Adams markets, unless compensating factors exist.

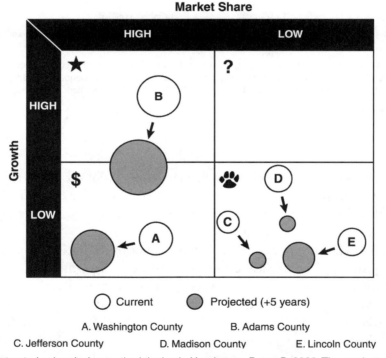

Constructed using design methodologies in Henderson, Bruce D. 2006. The product portfolio (1970). In the Boston Consulting Group on strategy: Classic concepts and new perspectives, 2nd ed., ed. Carl W. Stern and Michael S. Deimler. New York: Wiley.

FIGURE 5-3 A Thrift Shop's Growth/Share Matrix

Of course, in the nonprofit sector compensating factors are quite common. In the case of the rural medical center, perhaps there simply are no other options for primary care and wellness services in the community. In such cases, the medical center's mission might dictate that it continues pursuing weak product lines, whether prosperous or not.

In the case of the thrift shop, the weak stores might fill a critical gap in the given communities, providing options that would otherwise not exist. In other cases, patronage might very well have dwindled to the point that continued operations cannot be justified. Ceasing operations of the weak stores permits freed resources to be funneled into fewer stores, strengthening these outlets and affording greater aggregate benefits for served populations.

It is up to nonprofit executives themselves to make determinations as to which steps, if any, should be taken based on Growth/Share Matrix results. Importantly, even if goods and services cannot be shed from product portfolios due to prevailing missions, beliefs, or other circumstances, there is value in understanding where these offerings stand in the Growth/Share Matrix.

SUMMARY

The Boston Consulting Group's Growth/Share Matrix provides nonprofit executives with a simple, yet highly effective, portfolio analysis tool. Notably, the matrix assists nonprofit executives in their endeavors to assemble balanced product portfolios. Given the importance of assembling such portfolios, progressive nonprofit executives will find the Boston Consulting Group's Growth/Share Matrix to be an invaluable resource that greatly improves marketing efforts.

EXERCISES

1. Define and comprehensively discuss the Boston Consulting Group's Growth/Share Matrix, providing insights regarding its uses, features, methods of interpretation, and value, accompanied by an appropriate illustration. Be sure to include in your discussion an overview of the instrument's importance as a strategic marketing device in the nonprofit sector.

2. Contact a local nonprofit entity and arrange an informational interview with its top executive to discuss the organization's various product offerings. Explain the Boston Consulting Group's Growth/ Share Matrix, ask for insights as to how each of the noted offerings would be presented in the matrix, and prepare an associated illustration. Lastly, prepare a narrative discussing your experience.

REFERENCE

Henderson, B. D. (2006). The product portfolio, 1970. In C. W. Stern & M. S. Deimler (Eds.), *The Boston Consulting Group on strategy: Classic concepts and new perspectives* (2nd ed.) (pp. 35–37). New York, NY: Wiley.

General Electric's Strategic Business-Planning Grid

INTRODUCTION

Portfolio analysis, a rigorous endeavor entailing the comprehensive review of the goods and services offered by given establishments, is an essential marketing management activity. The reason that portfolio analysis is so essential is obvious: nonprofit executives must thoroughly understand their products if they are to successfully manage them.

The particular portfolio analysis tool used by nonprofit executives is dependent on the specific issues at hand and the level of analytical detail desired. Some portfolio analysis tools are very basic, while others are more sophisticated. One of the more elaborate portfolio analysis tools is known as the Strategic Business-Planning Grid, an evaluative device introduced by General Electric.

Illustrated in Figure 6-1, General Electric's Strategic Business-Planning Grid evaluates products based on industry attractiveness—here termed market attractiveness, which is more appropriate for the nonprofit sector—and business strength. Market attractiveness is a measure of a particular market's desirable attributes. Business strength is a measure of organization/product prowess, or lack thereof, in a particular market.

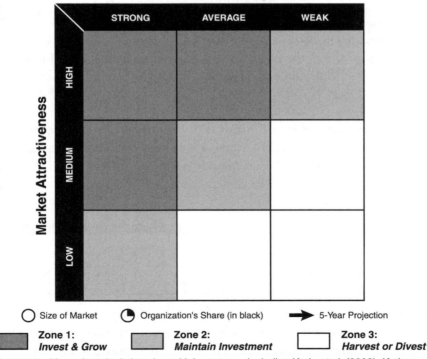

Constructed based on depictions in multiple sources, including Kerin et al. (2003), Kotler (2003), and Kotler and Armstrong (2001).

FIGURE 6-1 General Electric's Strategic Business-Planning Grid

General Electric's Strategic Business-Planning Grid consists of a vertical axis representing market attractiveness (high, medium, and low), a horizontal axis representing business strength (strong, average, and weak), and nine cells divided into three zones differentiated by color. Zone 1 encompasses the three cells located in the upper left corner of the grid. Products falling within these cells represent offerings that should receive further investment for growth. Zone 2 includes the three cells running diagonally from the lower left to upper right corners of the grid. For products falling within these cells, investment should be maintained. Zone 3 encompasses the three cells located in the lower right corner of the grid. Products falling within these cells represent drains on portfolios and should be harvested or divested, unless compensating factors exist.

The strength of General Electric's Strategic Business-Planning Grid rests with the fact that it is designed to incorporate multiple factors associated with attractiveness and strength. This multifactor feature allows nonprofit executives to develop axes that incorporate variables deemed most relevant to their particular operations. The result is a customized evaluative tool.

Variables that are commonly used to compose the attractiveness axis include market size, market growth, return on investment, and number of competitors. Variables that are commonly used to compose the strength axis include technological innovation, institutional capabilities, personnel, and distribution channels. The particular variables selected to compose each axis are completely up to the evaluating parties. The only requirement is that the selected variables appropriately relate to market attractiveness and business strength.

OPERATIONAL MATTERS

To assess products using General Electric's Strategic Business-Planning Grid, nonprofit executives (1) identify the product offerings they wish to evaluate; (2) construct the Strategic Business-Planning Grid, as illustrated in Figure 6-1; (3) determine the variables that will compose the attractiveness and strength axes, weighting variables as deemed appropriate if increased detail is desired; (4) gather relevant product and market data; and (5) plot each product on the diagram using circles that indicate market size, with larger circles indicating larger markets than smaller circles, and slices within each circle that indicate the market share of given offerings.

This visual representation is then analyzed to determine the strengths and weaknesses associated with given product portfolios. If additional detail is desired, nonprofit executives can use arrows to indicate anticipated attractiveness/strength characteristics.

Figure 6-2 identifies a Strategic Business-Planning Grid with forecast arrows that was developed for a community college. Here, the college evaluated its seven campuses—Georgetown, Colony, Northtown, Meadowbrook, Riverview, Midtown, and Oakdale—based on market attractiveness (defined by market size and market growth) and business strength (defined by campus location and degree offerings).

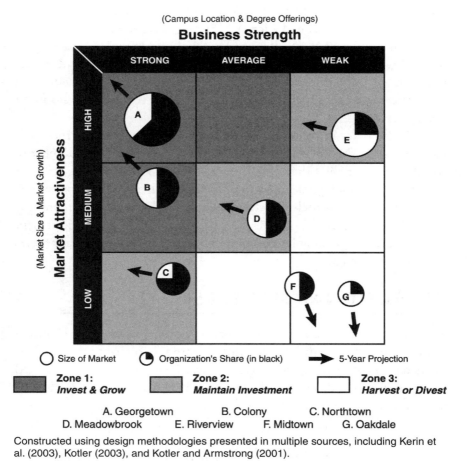

Constructed using design methodologies presented in multiple sources, including Kerin et al. (2003), Kotler (2003), and Kotler and Armstrong (2001).

FIGURE 6-2 A Community College's GE Grid

A review of the grid indicates that the community college currently has two Zone 1 offerings (i.e., Georgetown and Colony), three Zone 2 offerings (i.e., Northtown, Meadowbrook, and Riverview), and two Zone 3 offerings (i.e., Midtown and Oakdale). Of the establishments identified in Zone 1, Georgetown is most favorably situated, with Colony closely following. Given the combination of market attractiveness and business strength characteristics, the community college would be wise to invest further in these campuses in an effort to build these positions, especially given the positive five-year forecast, as indicated by the diagram's arrows.

Northtown, Meadowbrook, and Riverview are situated in Zone 2. These campuses deliver neither superior nor inferior performance; however, the five-year forecast indicates positive attractiveness/strength characteristics. Given their placement in Zone 2, coupled with the positive forecast, the community college would be wise to maintain its level of investment in these campuses.

Midtown and Oakdale are situated in Zone 3. These campuses possess inferior attractiveness/strength characteristics that are not expected to improve in the future. Unless compensating factors exist, these campuses should be eliminated from the community college's portfolio.

SUMMARY

General Electric's Strategic Business-Planning Grid provides nonprofit executives with a useful evaluative tool that can shed significant light on the product portfolios of organizations. With its ability to incorporate multiple variables into its attractiveness and strength axes, the grid offers a truly flexible device that can be customized to address almost any situation. Progressive nonprofit executives will undoubtedly find General Electric's Strategic Business-Planning Grid to be very useful in their endeavors to successfully manage product portfolios.

EXERCISES

1. Define and comprehensively discuss General Electric's Strategic Business-Planning Grid, its three associated zones, and methodology associated with placing products in the diagram. A diagram of the grid should be included to add value to your narrative. Be sure to include in your discussion details pertaining to how the particular

axes are formulated and the advantages associated with such. Share your thoughts regarding the tool's implications and uses in the non-profit sector.

2. Compare and contrast General Electric's Strategic Business-Planning Grid with the Boston Consulting Group's Growth/Share Matrix. Discuss the strengths and weaknesses of these two instruments. Share your thoughts on the particular tool you believe to be most appropriate for use in the nonprofit sector, providing justifications for your designated position.

REFERENCES

Kerin, R. A., Berkowitz, E. N., Hartley, S. W., & Rudelius, W. (2003). *Marketing* (7th ed.). New York, NY: McGraw-Hill.

Kotler, P. (2003). *Marketing management* (11th ed.). Upper Saddle River, NJ: Prentice Hall.

Kotler, P., & Armstrong, G. (2001). *Principles of marketing* (9th ed.). Upper Saddle River, NJ: Prentice Hall.

CHAPTER 7

Igor Ansoff's Product-Market Expansion Grid

LEARNING OBJECTIVES

After examining this chapter, readers will have the ability to:

- Recognize the importance of continually pursuing opportunities for growth in the marketplace.
- Understand that complacency, even for nonprofit entities occupying market leadership positions, will eventually lead to market share erosion and ultimately failure.
- Use Igor Ansoff's Product-Market Expansion Grid to identify expansion opportunities available to nonprofit organizations.
- Understand methods for gaining enhanced insights into growth prospects through the use of Igor Ansoff's Expansion Cube.

INTRODUCTION

The marketplace is characterized by constant change, intense competition, and general uncertainty. Given this turbulent environment, nonprofit executives must strive to proactively monitor their surroundings to, among other things, detect growth opportunities that can be pursued. Maintaining the status quo simply is not enough. Instead, nonprofit executives must vigorously pursue growth opportunities to increase the likelihood of

Products / Markets	Current	New
Current	*Market Penetration*	*Product Development*
New	*Market Development*	*Diversification*

Adapted from Corporate Strategy: An Analytic Approach to Business Policy for Growth and Expansion by H. Igor Ansoff. Copyright © 1965 by McGraw-Hill, Inc. Published by McGraw-Hill. Reprinted by permission of the estate of H. Igor Ansoff.

FIGURE 7-1 Ansoff's Product-Market Expansion Grid

institutional survival, growth, and prosperity. To capitalize on growth opportunities, nonprofit executives must carefully formulate appropriate expansion strategies—a process that is greatly facilitated by Igor Ansoff's Product-Market Expansion Grid.

Also known as Ansoff's Matrix, the Product-Market Expansion Grid was developed to shed light on the growth options available to organizations. Illustrated in Figure 7-1, the Product-Market Expansion Grid consists of a vertical axis representing markets (current and new), a horizontal axis representing products (current and new), and four cells that identify the four basic growth alternatives: market penetration, market development, product development, and diversification.

MARKET PENETRATION (CURRENT PRODUCTS, CURRENT MARKETS)

Market penetration is a growth strategy that seeks to increase the use of current product offerings by current customers. Here, growth is sought by identifying ways to increase consumption of the goods and services that are currently offered in existing markets. Marketing techniques used to achieve deeper market penetration include increased advertising, identification of new uses for products, price reductions, use of incentives, and so on. These techniques, when aimed at current markets, can stimulate consumption, resulting in increased growth.

MARKET DEVELOPMENT (CURRENT PRODUCTS, NEW MARKETS)

Market development is a growth strategy that involves the introduction of current products into new markets. This introduction is achieved by identifying new target audiences and directing current offerings accordingly. Current products may, for example, be placed in different geographic markets or directed toward new demographic segments to stimulate demand and increase growth. These new markets offer new opportunities to increase the consumption of current product offerings.

PRODUCT DEVELOPMENT (NEW PRODUCTS, CURRENT MARKETS)

Product development is a growth strategy that involves the introduction of new products into current markets. These products might be completely different offerings or they might be modified versions of existing products. With this strategy, nonprofit executives focus their efforts on developing new goods and services that will be attractive to current customers.

DIVERSIFICATION (NEW PRODUCTS, NEW MARKETS)

Diversification is a growth strategy that involves the introduction of new products into new markets. By focusing on new products and new markets, this strategy calls for organizations to enter completely unfamiliar territory. Given that both aspects of this pursuit—product and market—are new to organizations, diversification is the riskiest of the four growth strategies.

OPERATIONAL MATTERS

To formulate growth strategies using Ansoff's Product-Market Expansion Grid, nonprofit executives (1) construct the Product-Market Expansion Grid, as illustrated in Figure 7-1, (2) formulate growth options for each of the four growth strategies, and (3) place these growth options in their respective cells in the diagram. The resulting Product-Market Expansion Grid provides a simple, yet highly useful, depiction of available expansion opportunities.

Figure 7-2 identifies a Product-Market Expansion Grid that was developed for a workforce development center. Here, nonprofit executives could potentially achieve deeper market penetration than they currently have by increasing consumer awareness through expansion of the center's current advertising campaign. This more prominent campaign could direct more interest and attention toward the center and potentially increase its client base. Growth could also be achieved by developing a new geographic market through the placement of a branch office in a neighboring community.

Products / Markets	Current	New
Current	**Market Penetration** Expansion of the current advertising campaign	**Product Development** Introduction of a career mentoring program
New	**Market Development** Placement of a branch office in a neighboring community	**Diversification** Acquisition of a drug and alcohol treatment center

Constructed using design methodologies in Ansoff, H. Igor. 1965. Corporate strategy: An analytic approach to business policy for growth and expansion. New York: McGraw-Hill.

FIGURE 7-2 A Workforce Development Center's Expansion Grid

Another growth option involves the introduction of a career mentoring program to serve the current market. This new amenity could give the center a competitive advantage over other workforce development centers, increasing its customer base and providing added benefits that would be helpful to clients. Finally, the workforce development center could seek growth through diversification by purchasing and operating a drug and alcohol treatment center.

Figure 7-3 presents a Product-Market Expansion Grid that was developed for a municipal golf course. The golf course could potentially deepen its market penetration by organizing several on-site golf clinics that would encourage current and potential customers to play golf at the course. These events could build awareness in the market and ultimately increase patronage. Growth could also be achieved by targeting new demographic segments, encouraging them to visit the golf course. The golf course might, for example, develop an advertising campaign that targets minorities in an effort to attract associated patronage. To improve its position in the current market, the golf course could introduce a golf education and training

Products / Markets	Current	New
Current	**Market Penetration** On-site golf clinics to stimulate interest and attention	**Product Development** Introduction of a golf education and training center
New	**Market Development** Direction of promotional efforts to the minority population	**Diversification** Acquisition of a tennis and racquetball club

Constructed using design methodologies in Ansoff, H. Igor. 1965. Corporate strategy: An analytic approach to business policy for growth and expansion. New York: McGraw-Hill.

FIGURE 7-3 A Municipal Golf Course's Expansion Grid

center to serve clients who want to improve their golf skills. Lastly, the golf course could seek expansion through diversification by purchasing and operating a tennis and racquetball club.

It should be noted that although each strategy in the Product-Market Expansion Grid represents a distinct path toward growth, most organizations pursue multiple growth strategies simultaneously. Importantly, the Product-Market Expansion Grid does not communicate which strategy or strategies organizations should pursue. Instead, it focuses attention on the growth opportunities that are available to entities.

AN UPDATED VERSION

It should be mentioned that Igor Ansoff developed an updated version of his Product-Market Expansion Grid, which might be termed Ansoff's Expansion Cube. Illustrated in Figure 7-4, Ansoff's Expansion Cube incorporates three dimensions: market need, product technologies, and market geography. These three dimensions create a cube that illustrates

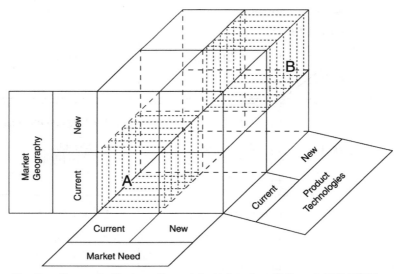

From The New Corporate Strategy, Rev. ed. by H. Igor Ansoff. Copyright © 1988 by H. Igor Ansoff. Published by John Wiley & Sons, Inc. Reprinted by permission of the estate of H. Igor Ansoff.

FIGURE 7-4 Ansoff's Expansion Cube

a variety of growth options, ranging from addressing current needs and current markets with current technologies (Section A) to addressing new needs and new markets with new technologies (Section B). Quite obviously, Ansoff's Expansion Cube offers enhanced insights into growth opportunities, making it highly useful for nonprofit executives seeking additional detail.

SUMMARY

The long-term viability of nonprofit organizations largely depends on the successful identification and pursuit of growth opportunities. Igor Ansoff's Product-Market Expansion Grid provides nonprofit executives with a very powerful and effective tool for recognizing and evaluating these opportunities. This tool greatly assists nonprofit executives in the development of appropriate expansion strategies.

EXERCISES

1. Compare and contrast Igor Ansoff's Product-Market Expansion Grid with his Expansion Cube, identifying the components of each, supported by illustrations. Which model possesses the most utility for use in the nonprofit sector? Why do you view this to be the case?
2. Select a local nonprofit entity and gain insights into its current array of product offerings. Based on your knowledge of the market and this local establishment, formulate one growth option for each of the four growth strategies identified in Igor Ansoff's Product-Market Expansion Grid. Identify the particular option you believe to be most viable. Be sure to provide justifications for your selection.

REFERENCES

Ansoff, H. I. (1965). *Corporate strategy: An analytic approach to business policy for growth and expansion.* New York, NY: McGraw-Hill.
Ansoff, H. I. (1988). *The new corporate strategy* (Rev. ed.). New York, NY: Wiley.

PART II

Branding and Identity Management Tools

CHAPTER **8**

Schmitt and Simonson's Drivers of Identity Management

LEARNING OBJECTIVES

After examining this chapter, readers will have the ability to:
- Understand the critical pursuit of identity management and its role in helping nonprofit entities build strong, recognizable brands.
- Realize the importance of establishing brands and other elements of identity as a means of differentiating given products from competitive offerings in the marketplace.
- Appreciate the value and guidance offered by Schmitt and Simonson's Drivers of Identity Management as a tool for informing nonprofit executives of the circumstances that necessitate addressing elements of identity within their given institutions.

INTRODUCTION

Nonprofit executives must continually be concerned with how their organizations and related product offerings are perceived by target audiences. The efforts of nonprofit executives in the creation of desirable identities for their product offerings can influence customer perceptions.

Table 8-1 Schmitt and Simonson's Drivers of Identity Management

1. Change in corporate structure
2. Low loyalty or losing share
3. Outdated image
4. Inconsistent image
5. New products and product extensions
6. New competitors
7. Changing customers
8. Entry into new markets
9. Greater resources

Source: Derived from information in Schmitt, B., & Simonson, A. (1997). *Marketing aesthetics: The strategic management of brands, identity, and image.* New York, NY: The Free Press.

Identity is achieved through branding activities, specifically, generating logos, product names, slogans, jingles, product packaging, building signage, and related identity vehicles for the purpose of conveying the desired images to target audiences. Branding activities assist customers in identifying goods and services in the marketplace, helping them to distinguish products from the competitive offerings. Attending to these activities is often termed *identity management*, which is one of the most important responsibilities of nonprofit executives.

Given the importance of identity management activities, it is helpful for nonprofit executives to possess an understanding of the primary forces that drive such efforts. To aid in achieving this understanding, Bernd Schmitt and Alex Simonson identified nine drivers of identity management, which are illustrated in Table 8-1. These nine drivers—change in corporate structure, low loyalty or losing share, outdated image, inconsistent image, new products and product extensions, new competitors, changing customers, entry into new markets, and greater resources—are defined as follows.

CHANGE IN CORPORATE STRUCTURE

Alterations in the corporate structures of establishments are quite common across all industries. Mergers and acquisitions, for example, occur for any number of reasons, but both are prefaced by the belief that combined, rather than singular, efforts will yield enhanced benefits for the organizations under examination.

Any time two or more nonprofit organizations combine to form a single establishment, identity management issues must be addressed. Possibly the most pressing identity management issue associated with mergers and acquisitions is the determination of an appropriate name for the newly combined entity. Should the two organizations be allowed to carry their existing, separate identities (e.g., Ridgewood Community Center *and* Washington Recreational Pavilion)? Should the two establishments agree to accept one name over the other (e.g., Ridgewood Community Center)? Should the entities select some sort of a hybrid name (e.g., Ridgewood-Washington Center)?

These questions may or may not be easy to answer depending on the particular circumstances associated with the given transactions. Factors to consider include the strength or weakness of given brand names, the real or anticipated preferences of target markets, and so on—issues that must be thoroughly investigated prior to making such determinations.

As with mergers and acquisitions, spin-offs elicit an equally intensive need for identity management activities. Clearly, changes in the corporate structures of nonprofit organizations serve as drivers of identity management.

LOW LOYALTY OR LOSING SHARE

Customer loyalty is an essential ingredient for marketing success. Loyalty not only delivers the benefits associated with customer retention but also results in customers echoing their support to members of their social circles, participating in the very powerful communications medium of word-of-mouth publicity. Customer loyalty bolsters market share, increasing the likelihood of growth and prosperity.

Naturally, low customer loyalty and market share attrition are causes of concern for any nonprofit executive, and such occurrences may, at least in part, be the result of identity problems. Valuable identities are the result of brand characteristics that are attractive to target audiences and strategically well managed. Nonprofit establishments must ensure that they possess such identities.

OUTDATED IMAGE

Brand imagery, with the passage of time, is subject to stagnation in the eyes of customers. Simply stated, diminished imagery equates with diminished identity and thus serves as a driver of identity management. It is prudent to periodically review all elements of identity from time to time to ensure that the image continues to be current in the eyes of customers and to refresh the branding elements as necessary.

INCONSISTENT IMAGE

Consistency in the imagery associated with identity is a must. Ideally, logos, building signage, promotional materials, and so on should be coordinated to achieve a consistent, orderly appearance. Unfortunately, such consistency is not always the case.

Inconsistent imagery is confusing to customers, resulting in difficulties in identifying given establishments and their product offerings. It also typically conveys the impression of disorder—a disastrous image for any organization.

NEW PRODUCTS AND PRODUCT EXTENSIONS

When new products and product extensions are introduced into the marketplace, identity creation decisions are required. Such decisions range from being very simple to being very complex, depending on the nature of the new offering and its placement within a given product portfolio.

A community tennis club would not encounter a very rigorous identity creation decision if it decided to simply enhance its existing array of offerings by, say, adding a pro shop. If, instead, the tennis club decided to enter a completely different athletic arena by, say, constructing an adjacent swimming center, the identity creation decision would be much more difficult. Regardless of the level of difficulty involved in creating effective identities, new products and product extensions clearly hasten the identity management process.

NEW COMPETITORS

Identity management is one of many activities that nonprofit executives must engage in when new competitors enter the market. Among other things, new competitors bring their new identities into the marketplace, and these identities might impact consumer perceptions of existing ones in the given environment. Such competitive entry minimally calls for nonprofit executives to review their existing identity management efforts and may call for the alteration and enhancement of given identities. Ultimately, nonprofit executives would like for their identities to be viewed more favorably than their competitors by consumers, making the introduction of new competitors into the marketplace a driver of identity management.

CHANGING CUSTOMERS

Customers, their wants and needs, their tastes and preferences, their perceptions, and their environments are constantly changing. In an effort to stay relevant in the minds of customers, the identities of establishments and their product offerings must change in tandem with changing customers.

On an ongoing basis, nonprofit executives must study their desired customer populations and objectively analyze their identity management efforts, seeking to view such efforts from the perspective of target audiences. By doing this, nonprofit executives stay abreast of changing customer characteristics, allowing them to alter identities accordingly to meet the current expectations of target markets.

ENTRY INTO NEW MARKETS

Whenever organizations enter new markets, identity management efforts must carefully be evaluated. Here, nonprofit executives must determine whether to use existing identities, related identities, or entirely new identities in these new markets. Because different markets quite frequently possess different characteristics, existing identity schemes may not be transferable to new settings. This fact necessitates that nonprofit executives carefully investigate identity management issues associated with newly targeted markets and design their identities accordingly.

GREATER RESOURCES

Burgeoning resources afford nonprofit executives with more identity options (e.g., more appealing facility signage, more elaborate product packaging, enhanced marketing communications initiatives) which are worthy of exploration in attempts to build customer perceptions regarding given product offerings. Whenever an infusion of resources occurs (e.g., more prosperous economic periods, greater donor generosity), nonprofit executives must comprehensively review their identity management efforts to determine the most productive methods for utilizing these funds to effect the greatest identity gains possible in the marketplace.

SUMMARY

Because marketing success requires effective identity management efforts, nonprofit executives must ensure that they are aware of the circumstances and events that drive such endeavors. The typology offered by Schmitt and Simonson effectively portrays the forces that drive identity management, reminding nonprofit executives of their important responsibilities.

EXERCISES

1. Provide a detailed overview of Schmitt and Simonson's Drivers of Identity Management, noting facets regarding its purpose, use, and value in nonprofit entities. Share your thoughts and ideas regarding the degree to which modern nonprofit organizations should actively engage in routine endeavors to ensure appropriate identities.
2. Select a nonprofit organization in your local market and study its logo and other elements of brand identity. Using guidance provided by Schmitt and Simonson's Drivers of Identity Management regarding inconsistent imagery, prepare a report detailing the degree to which you believe the selected facility's logo and associated branding elements convey an image of consistency and order. If you believe that changes are necessary, what do you recommend? If you believe that changes are not necessary, why do you consider this to be the case?

REFERENCE

Schmitt, B., & Simonson, A. (1997). *Marketing aesthetics: The strategic management of brands, identity, and image.* New York, NY: The Free Press.

Calder and Reagan's Brand Design Model

INTRODUCTION

Brands are names, logos, slogans, and other references that identify goods and services, thus allowing customers to distinguish products from competitive offerings. In essence, brands give products *identity*, a component that is absolutely essential for the purpose of product differentiation.

Brands can be used to identify individual products, product lines, or entire organizations, and they benefit both producers and consumers, as presented in Figure 9-1. These benefits illustrate the critical importance of brands, making the successful establishment of brand identity one of the most essential tasks of marketing management.

Despite the importance of branding, the process of brand development is often conducted in an unsystematic, haphazard fashion, typically as a derivative of either marketing plans or advertising. In an effort to bring order to this process and improve branding results, Bobby Calder and Steven Reagan developed the Brand Design Model.

Illustrated in Figure 9-2, the Brand Design Model consists of an inner circle representing the meaningful relevant value of a product and an outer circle representing verbal and visual brand expressions. The Brand Design Model challenges nonprofit executives to first identify product-related meaning (i.e., meaningful relevant value) and then formulate methods to convey this meaning to customers through an arrangement of verbal and visual elements (i.e., brand expressions). Meaningful relevant value and brand expressions of the Brand Design Model are explained as follows.

FIGURE 9-1 Functions of a Brand

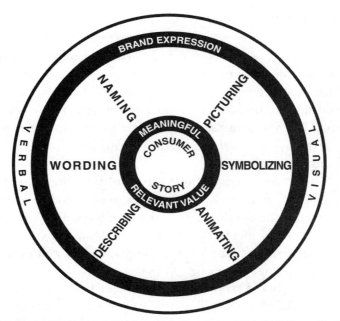

From "Brand Design" by Bobby J. Calder and Steven J. Reagan in Kellogg on Marketing, edited by Dawn Iacobucci. Copyright © 2001 by John Wiley & Sons, Inc. Reprinted with permission of John Wiley & Sons, Inc.

FIGURE 9-2 Calder & Reagan's Brand Design Model

MEANINGFUL RELEVANT VALUE

Through branding, nonprofit executives seek to make products more meaningful to customers, and one of the best methods for accomplishing this goal entails viewing products from the perspective of target markets. To view products through the eyes of customers, nonprofit executives must ask themselves how their products positively impact the lives of customers. When viewing products in this manner, nonprofit executives focus their attention on the prime motivator of consumer purchase activity—the ability of products to satisfy wants and needs. These inquiries ultimately yield consumer stories that are meaningful to target markets. When consumer stories have been formulated, nonprofit executives then focus on conveyance of these stories to target markets through the formulation of brand expressions.

BRAND EXPRESSIONS

Brands can be expressed using verbal and visual elements. Verbal brand expressions include naming (i.e., the assignment of names to products), wording (i.e., the development of specialized vocabularies, such as catch phrases and slogans, to describe product attributes), and describing (i.e., the scripting of phrases and sentences that elaborate upon the attributes of products, such as product uses, safety information, durability information, or customer testimonials).

Visual brand expressions include picturing (i.e., the presentation of products using still photography and other static, illustrative methods), symbolizing (i.e., the development and use of logos and other abstract, symbolic methods to identify products), and animating (i.e., the use of "moving" pictures, including video photography and computer animation, to present products).

In formulating brand expressions, the ultimate goal is to develop verbal and visual components that will accurately convey the meaning of products—the consumer stories revealed through meaningful relevant value inquiries—to target markets.

OPERATIONAL MATTERS

To develop brands using Calder and Reagan's Brand Design Model, nonprofit executives should (1) identify the product to be branded, (2) construct the brand design diagram, as illustrated in Figure 9-2, (3) identify and/or formulate a product-related story that is of interest to target markets along with verbal and visual brand expressions that will convey this story to customers, and (4) place these elements on the brand design diagram accordingly. The resulting diagram yields a customer-focused brand identity for the given product offering.

Figure 9-3 illustrates a Brand Design Model that was developed for a newly established automobile association. Here, the association has identified a relevant story of consumer interest—the peace of mind associated with safe automobile transportation courtesy of a comprehensive, national roadside assistance network—and has designed its verbal and visual expressions around this story. Quite clearly, each verbal and visual element directly relates to the safety and security afforded to drivers who purchase a membership with the automobile association. Courtesy of the Brand

Design Model, the association has successfully formulated a customer-focused brand identity that will allow it to effectively market automobile travel support services to its target audience. Coordinated promotional efforts can now be initiated.

The automobile association's completed schematic illustrates the power of the Brand Design Model. In one simple diagram, nonprofit executives can view the strategic and tactical brand fundamentals associated with given product offerings. This centralized source of carefully prepared information is particularly useful in achieving consistency of presentation across advertising media. Given the increasing array of available media, along with the desire for more precise target marketing, the Brand Design Model offers nonprofit executives a method for ensuring integrated marketing communications.

It should be noted that the Brand Design Model is to be formulated in an inclusive fashion where input from all organizational members

Constructed using design methodologies in Calder, Bobby J., and Steven J. Reagan. 2001. Brand design. In Kellogg on marketing, ed. Dawn Iacobucci. New York: Wiley.

FIGURE 9-3 An Automobile Association's Brand Design Model

involved in the development and management of associated products is actively encouraged. The multiple perspectives offered by this extended group of individuals can greatly enhance resulting brand designs.

SUMMARY

Brands allow customers to distinguish goods and services from competitive offerings and are, therefore, essential for the purpose of product differentiation. Given the importance of brands, nonprofit executives can significantly benefit from the branding process offered by Calder and Reagan's Brand Design Model.

The Brand Design Model guides nonprofit executives through the process of formulating brands that convey customer-focused meaning—an absolute requirement for attracting the patronage of target markets. Despite its simplicity, the Brand Design Model significantly enhances branding results. Progressive nonprofit executives will undoubtedly find it to be an invaluable resource that greatly improves marketing efforts.

EXERCISES

1. Provide a detailed overview of Calder and Reagan's Brand Design Model, illustrating its use and value as a device for systematically guiding nonprofit executives through the process of formulating brands. Share your perspectives regarding the degree to which nonprofit organizations in your local community are communicating consistent messages across their various communications platforms.
2. Place yourself in the role of a nonprofit entrepreneur who is contemplating the development of a good, service, or institution of your choice. Using Calder and Reagan's Brand Design Model, create this particular item's consumer story, assemble verbal and visual brand expressions, and place these elements in an appropriate brand design diagram. Provide a brief narrative explaining your thoughts and ideas.

REFERENCES

Berthon, P., Hulbert, J. M., & Pitt, L. F. (1999). Brand management prognostications. *MIT Sloan Management Review, 40*(2), 53–65.

Calder, B. J., & Reagan, S. J. (2001). Brand design. In D. Iacobucci (Ed.), *Kellogg on marketing* (pp. 58–73). New York, NY: Wiley.

Martin Lindstrom's 5-D Brand Sensogram

INTRODUCTION

Successful branding initiatives result in the establishment of appropriate and effective identities and associated representations (e.g., names, logos, slogans, and other identifiers) for nonprofit organizations and the products they offer to target audiences. Because brands are used by customers to recognize goods and services and to distinguish them from competitive offerings, the importance of branding and associated identity management activities cannot be understated.

Brands have traditionally been viewed as verbal and visual manifestations that are designed and developed to represent organizations and their product offerings. While verbal and visual elements are, and will continue to be, core components for the establishment of institutional and product identity, such attributes only tap into the sight (i.e., visual) and sound (i.e., verbal) senses. The remaining senses—taste, touch, and smell—have largely gone unaddressed in branding, but represent potential opportunities for nonprofit executives to further distinguish their offerings.

An understanding of the brand enrichment opportunities afforded by addressing the five senses led Martin Lindstrom to suggest moving beyond the traditional, two-dimensional (2-D) view of branding and, instead, embrace a more comprehensive, five-dimensional (5-D) perspective that incorporates all five senses—sight, sound, taste, touch, and smell—providing enhanced opportunities to communicate with customers.

To assist brand designers in their efforts to formulate 5-D brands, Lindstrom developed the 5-D Brand Sensogram. As illustrated in Figure 10-1, the Brand Sensogram is depicted as a pentagon with each

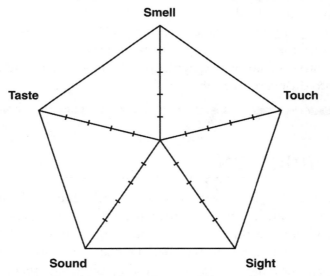

FIGURE 10-1 Lindstrom's 5-D Brand Sensogram

point identifying a different sense—sight, sound, taste, touch, and smell. Five-point scales running from the center of the diagram outward to associated points indicate the strength of given senses pertaining to the brand under examination, with greater distance from the center indicating greater strength. Prefaced by descriptions of the five senses of sight, sound, taste, touch, and smell, Lindstrom's 5-D Brand Sensogram is explained as follows.

SIGHT

Sight-related brand manifestations include logos, slogans, illustrations, and photographs, along with the marketing communications devices that incorporate these items, including business cards, facility signage, product packaging, and visual advertisements. Beyond items that are traditionally associated with marketing communications, however, numerous other sight-related branding opportunities are available. Such possibilities include institutional cleanliness; well-groomed, appropriately attired employees; attractive landscaping; and well-appointed reception areas, office spaces, and conference rooms. These sight-related elements of branding, if designed effectively, have the potential to positively impact customers and their perceptions of nonprofit institutions.

SOUND

Sound-related brand manifestations include jingles, musical scores, and customer testimonials, along with the marketing communications tools that incorporate these items, including music-on-hold programming, corporate sound systems, and audio advertisements. Sound offers nonprofit entities many creative branding opportunities. Original promotional tunes, for example, can play when office computers boot up or they can be converted into ringtones for employee-issued cellular telephones. Both would bolster the brand identity of the given nonprofit establishments.

TASTE

Taste represents a departure from the traditional sight and sound mindset of branding, but opportunities, under the right circumstances, clearly exist for taste to bolster brands. School cafeterias are often said to serve food that is not particularly desirable, affording these entities with opportunities to bolster consumer perceptions by ensuring that food service departments endeavor to prepare excellent meals for students and faculty.

Beyond entities that are in the business of delivering taste-oriented products, opportunities exist to incorporate taste elements to bolster brands that have nothing to do with taste. A civic club, for example, might decide to hold an annual fish fry to reward existing members and recruit new ones. A museum might provide free cappuccinos to patrons. These subtle taste-oriented elements can greatly facilitate brand identity for the associated organizations. While achieving taste-related brand characteristics is not possible in all circumstances, nonprofit executives are encouraged to take advantage of such opportunities when they present themselves.

TOUCH

As with taste, touch represents a nontraditional characteristic of branding with much potential to bolster identity in certain situations. Zoological parks, for example, have many opportunities to incorporate touch-related elements. Exhibits permitting patrons to interact with animals, holding and petting them, represents a very obvious touch-related example. Libraries can incorporate quality furnishings and fixtures that are pleasing to the touch for their patron populations.

Beyond some of the more obvious opportunities, facets of touch can be incorporated in details as minute as using a higher grade of paper for business cards and stationery. Customers indeed notice these subtle elements. Each of these facets illustrates the use of touch as an opportunity to bolster the brand identity efforts of nonprofit organizations.

SMELL

The nontraditional brand manifestation of smell affords nonprofit entities with a wealth of opportunities to bolster brand identity efforts. Hospitals, medical centers, and nursing homes are highly concerned with maintaining good air quality—a smell-related element—to establish perceptions of safe and clean clinical environments. These establishments are equally concerned with ensuring that linens possess fresh scents that further bolster cleanliness initiatives.

An example that perhaps more readily comes to mind concerning smell would be the public restrooms at virtually any nonprofit establishment (e.g., campgrounds, parks, workforce development centers). Expectations may be low, providing opportunities for nonprofit organizations to pleasantly surprise patrons by providing clean, fresh environments. The sense of smell influences customer perceptions of nonprofit entities and their product offerings, making smell an important element in the establishment of brand identity.

THE 5-D BRAND SENSOGRAM

Lindstrom's 5-D Brand Sensogram permits the measurement of institutional efforts at establishing 5-D brands. To do this, nonprofit executives (1) identify the product offering to be evaluated; (2) construct the Brand Sensogram, as illustrated in Figure 10-1; (3) rank the offering's brand characteristics related to each of the five senses, plotting discoveries on the diagram accordingly; and (4) connect the plotted points. This visual representation is then analyzed to determine the given brand's sensory awareness properties, allowing nonprofit executives the opportunity to bolster their identity management efforts.

Enhanced insights can be afforded by noting the specific brand characteristics that prompted the rankings in completed Brand Sensograms. Additional detail can be gained by plotting competitive brands over completed Brand Sensograms to comparatively assess branding initiatives.

As Figures 10-2 and 10-3 illustrate, completion of this simple diagram yields considerable insights into efforts to establish multidimensional brands and hence serves as an essential brand management tool.

SUMMARY

Lindstrom's 5-D Brand Sensogram draws significant attention to the multidimensional nature of brands, affording nonprofit executives with a convenient tool for assessing their efforts to incorporate sight, sound, taste, touch, and smell into their goods and services. By addressing each of the senses within Lindstrom's 5-D Brand Sensogram, nonprofit executives can deliver enriched product offerings that are attractive to target audiences on many levels.

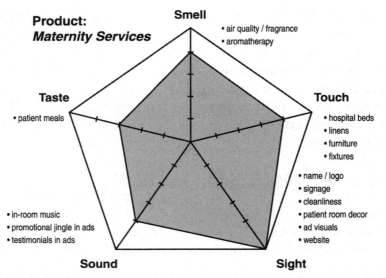

Constructed using design methodologies in Lindstrom, Martin. 2005. Brand sense: Build powerful brands through touch, taste, smell, sight, and sound. New York: The Free Press.

FIGURE 10-2 A Hospital's 5-D Brand Sensogram

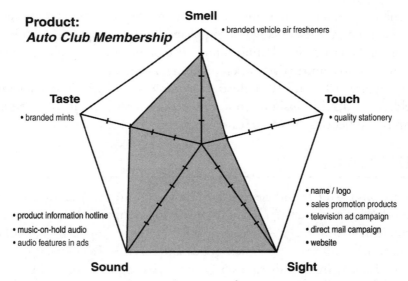

Constructed using design methodologies in Lindstrom, Martin. 2005. Brand sense: Build powerful brands through touch, taste, smell, sight, and sound. New York: The Free Press.

FIGURE 10-3 An Automobile Club's 5-D Brand Sensogram

EXERCISES

1. Define and comprehensively discuss Martin Lindstrom's 5-D Brand Sensogram, providing insights into the five dimensional realms of sight, sound, taste, touch, and smell. Share your thoughts regarding the tool's implications and uses in the nonprofit sector. Provide your perspectives regarding the degree to which you believe modern nonprofit entities address each of the five dimensions.

2. Select a local nonprofit entity and arrange to visit the organization. On your tour of the facility, look for identity elements that relate to the five senses of sight, sound, taste, touch, and smell. With this information, prepare a 5-D Brand Sensogram for the establishment. Are branding opportunities available? If so, how might you address these opportunities in a manner to maximize identity?

REFERENCE

Lindstrom, M. (2005). *Brand sense: Build powerful brands through touch, taste, smell, sight, and sound.* New York, NY: The Free Press.

CHAPTER 11

Lederer and Hill's Brand Portfolio Molecule

LEARNING OBJECTIVES

After examining this chapter, readers will have the ability to:

- Understand that brands exist not in isolation but in a larger environment that includes other brands.
- Realize that brands impact one another; sometimes positively, sometimes neutrally, and sometimes negatively.
- Appreciate the value of Lederer and Hill's Brand Portfolio Molecule as a tool for understanding brand relationships.

INTRODUCTION

Brands are names, logos, slogans, and other identifiers that are developed and assigned to products to help customers distinguish goods and services from competitive offerings. By successfully branding products, nonprofit executives greatly increase the likelihood that customers will recognize their goods and services—an essential prerequisite for purchase activity.

Given the obvious importance of branding, nonprofit executives must work diligently to ensure that they understand the brands they are responsible for managing. The better nonprofit executives understand brands, the better prepared they will be to appropriately manage these offerings.

One of the most effective tools for understanding brands is known as the Brand Portfolio Molecule which, as illustrated in Figure 11-1, presents brand portfolios in the form of atoms. Developed by Chris Lederer and Sam Hill, the Brand Portfolio Molecule multidimensionally illustrates the relationships that exist among brands within given product portfolios. The Brand Portfolio Molecule also identifies, in the same multidimensional fashion, associated external brands that impact these portfolios.

COMPONENTS OF THE BRAND PORTFOLIO MOLECULE

A Brand Portfolio Molecule consists of a large central atom (i.e., the lead brand) that represents the most influential brand within a given portfolio; midsized atoms (i.e., strategic brands), which heavily influence customer purchases; and small atoms (i.e., support brands), which mildly influence customer purchases.

The color of atoms in the Brand Portfolio Molecule indicates the influence that particular brands have within given portfolios. A light color indicates a positive influence, a medium color indicates a neutral influence, and a dark color indicates a negative influence.

Nodes are atoms (i.e., brands) that have relationships with other atoms (i.e., brands), with direct connections indicating direct relationships and indirect connections indicating indirect relationships. The width of the link between nodes indicates the degree of control that one brand commands over the other. Thicker links indicate greater control than thin links do.

Proximity indicates the positioning characteristics of brands. Brands that are close in proximity are similarly positioned. Brands that are more distant in proximity are more distinctly positioned.

OPERATIONAL MATTERS

To assemble a Brand Portfolio Molecule, nonprofit executives (1) list all the brands within a given portfolio, as well as associated external brands; (2) classify each brand as lead, strategic, or support; (3) establish the network of relationships that exist among these brands; and (4) map the Brand Portfolio Molecule either by hand or with the assistance of illustration software. When mapped, nonprofit executives use the Brand Portfolio Molecule to assess given brand portfolios.

Figure 11-1 illustrates a Brand Portfolio Molecule that was developed for a community sports complex. From the molecule, it is easily determined that Westport Sports Complex is the lead brand because it is the largest atom in the diagram. Westport Sports Complex is positively influenced by its "Westport for Sports" slogan and its Blue Ribbon Fitness accreditation. The entity is neutrally influenced by its hosting of the Capital City Baseball Championship. Westport Sports Complex serves as the umbrella brand for three distinct units that provide positive influences: Westport Sports Instruction, Westport Sports Nutrition, and Westport Sports Rehabilitation.

Westport Sports Instruction is positively influenced by its relationship with its parent, Westport Sports Complex, as well as the annual tennis clinic that it holds for community residents. Westport Sports Nutrition is positively influenced by its relationship with Westport Sports Complex and neutrally influenced by its relationship with City College's Nutritional Sciences Department. Westport Sports Rehabilitation is positively influenced by its relationship with Westport Sports Complex, its distribution of *The Road to Recovery Newsletter*, and its "Back in Action" program that is offered to various patrons. Westport Sports Rehabilitation is neutrally influenced by its sponsorship of the Capital City Health Fair.

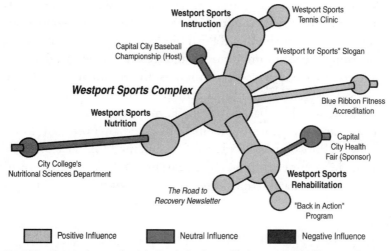

Constructed using design methodologies in Lederer, Chris, and Sam Hill. 2001. See your brands through your customers' eyes. Harvard Business Review (June): 125–133.

FIGURE 11-1 A Sports Complex's Brand Portfolio Molecule

The Brand Portfolio Molecule clearly illustrates that Westport Sports Complex possesses a strong array of brands, with positive influences dominating its portfolio. The complex is particularly fortunate not to have any brands that negatively influence the portfolio. With this information, Westport Sports Complex can focus its attention on maintaining the numerous positive components of its brand portfolio.

SUMMARY

Lederer and Hill's Brand Portfolio Molecule provides nonprofit executives with a valuable tool for understanding the relationships that exist within brand portfolios. By clearly demonstrating internal brand relationships, as well as relationships that exist with associated external brands, the Brand Portfolio Molecule allows nonprofit executives to identify strong, neutral, and weak points associated with their brands. With its succinct presentation of given brand portfolios and associated relationships, the Brand Portfolio Molecule facilitates brand management activities.

EXERCISES

1. Provide a detailed overview of Lederer and Hill's Brand Portfolio Molecule, identifying and explaining its assembly methods, its features, and its benefits. Support this overview by drawing an example illustration of the Brand Portfolio Molecule. Share your thoughts regarding the tool's implications and uses in the nonprofit sector.
2. Assume that you have been hired as an administrative officer for a newly established nondenominational church, known as Peace Church, which is based in your hometown. After studying your local market to gain insights into the given environment, assemble a Brand Portfolio Molecule for Peace Church. As Peace Church is in its developmental stages, concentrate only on potential relationships with external brands. Provide a brief narrative explaining your illustration.

REFERENCE

Lederer, C., & Hill, S. (2001, June). See your brands through your customers' eyes. *Harvard Business Review, 79,* 125–133.

Kevin Lane Keller's Brand Report Card

INTRODUCTION

Branding—the development, assignment, and management of names, logos, slogans, and other identifiers associated with products—is one of the most important activities of nonprofit marketing management. Through branding, nonprofit executives give their products *identity*. This identity allows customers to distinguish goods and services from competitive offerings.

Branding activities do not cease with the introduction of products into the marketplace. Instead, these activities are ongoing. Consumers, their wants and needs, their preferences, their perceptions, and their environments are constantly changing. Brands and the products they represent must keep up with these changes—a task which necessitates that nonprofit executives devote significant attention to branding throughout the product life cycle.

Given the dynamic nature of the marketplace and its consumers, nonprofit executives must periodically assess the brand performance of their offerings in an effort to ensure that brands are meeting strategic and tactical goals and objectives. To aid in the process of brand evaluation, Kevin Lane Keller developed the Brand Report Card, a useful tool that allows nonprofit executives to evaluate their offerings based on 10 characteristics possessed by excellent brands.

Illustrated in Figure 12-1, Keller's Brand Report Card requires that nonprofit executives (1) read each of the 10 brand characteristics; (2) rate their brands on a scale of 1 to 10 for each characteristic, with 1 being extremely poor and 10 being extremely good; and (3) create a bar chart that reflects the results of the evaluation. This chart is then analyzed to determine strengths and weaknesses associated with brand management. The 10 characteristics possessed by excellent brands are identified as follows.

CHARACTERISTIC 1

The brand excels at delivering the benefits customers truly desire.
When customers purchase products, they are buying collections of tangible and intangible attributes that satisfy wants and needs. In arranging these tangible and intangible characteristics, nonprofit executives must strive to ensure that their products incorporate the attributes that customers indeed are seeking. This, of course, first requires the identification of the particular product attributes desired and required by customers.

Identification of such attributes can be accomplished through a variety of methods. One such method is known as environmental scanning, an externally focused activity where nonprofit executives seek to assess the environment in an effort to identify marketplace trends. Externally focused activities are ideally supplemented by internally focused activities. One example of an internally focused activity is the customer satisfaction survey,

Rating Your Brand

Instructions: Rate your brand on a scale of one to ten (one being extremely poor and ten being extremely good) for each characteristic below. Then create a bar chart that reflects the scores. Use the bar chart to generate discussion among all those individuals who participate in the management of your brands. Looking at the results in that manner should help you identify areas that need improvement, recognize areas in which you excel, and learn more about how your particular brand is configured.

It can also be helpful to create a report card and chart for competitors' brands simply by rating those brands based on your own perceptions, both as a competitor and as a consumer. As an outsider, you may know more about how their brands are received in the marketplace than they do.

Keep that in mind as you evaluate your own brand. Try to look at it through the eyes of consumers rather than through your own knowledge of budgets, teams, and time spent on various initiatives.

The brand excels at delivering the benefits customers truly desire.

Have you attempted to uncover unmet consumer wants and needs? By what methods? Do you focus relentlessly on maximizing your customers' product experiences? Do you have a system in place for getting comments from customers to the people who can effect change?

The brand stays relevant.

Have you invested in product improvements that provide better value for your customers? Are you in touch with your customers' tastes? With the current market conditions? With new trends as they apply to your offering? Are your marketing decisions based on your knowledge of the above?

The pricing strategy is based on customers' perceptions of value.

Have you optimized price, cost, and quality to meet or exceed customers' expectations? Do you have a system in place to monitor customers' perceptions of your brand's value? Have you estimated how much value your customers believe the brand adds to your product?

The brand is properly positioned.

Have you established necessary and competitive points of parity with competitors? Have you established desirable and deliverable points of difference?

The brand is consistent.

Are you sure that your marketing programs are not sending conflicting messages and that they haven't done so over time? Conversely, are you adjusting your programs to keep current?

FIGURE 12-1 Keller's Brand Report Card (*Continued*)

The brand portfolio and hierarchy make sense.

Can the corporate brand create a seamless umbrella for all brands in the portfolio? Do the brands in that portfolio hold individual niches? How extensively do the brands overlap? In what areas? Conversely, do the brands maximize market coverage? Do you have a brand hierarchy that is well thought out and well understood?

The brand makes use of and coordinates a full repertoire of marketing activities to build equity.

Have you chosen or designed your brand name, logo, symbol, slogan, packaging, signage, and so forth to maximize brand awareness? Have you implemented integrated marketing activities that target customers? Are you aware of all the marketing activities that involve your brand? Are the people managing each activity aware of one another? Have you capitalized on the unique capabilities of each communication option while ensuring that the meaning of the brand is consistently represented?

The brand's managers understand what the brand means to customers.

Do you know what customers like and don't like about a brand? Are you aware of all the core associations people make with your brand, whether intentionally created by your organization or not? Have you created detailed, research-driven portraits of your target customers? Have you outlined customer-driven boundaries for brand extensions and guidelines for marketing programs?

The brand is given proper support and that support is sustained over the long run.

Are the successes or failures of marketing programs fully understood before they are changed? Is the brand given sufficient R&D support? Have you avoided the temptation to cut back marketing support for the brand in reaction to a downturn in the market or a slump in sales?

The organization monitors sources of brand equity.

Have you created a brand charter that defines the meaning and equity of the brand and how it should be treated? Do you conduct periodic brand audits to assess the health of your brand and to set strategic direction? Do you conduct routine tracking studies to evaluate current market performance? Do you regularly distribute brand equity reports that summarize all relevant research and information to assist marketers in making decisions? Have you assigned explicit responsibility for monitoring and preserving brand equity?

FIGURE 12-1 Keller's Brand Report Card

which requests feedback from customers regarding their experiences, perceptions, and opinions concerning the ability of organizations to appropriately address wants and needs.

Identification of customer wants and needs is, however, only part of the equation. The other part, of course, involves the development and delivery of innovative product solutions that satisfy the identified wants and needs.

CHARACTERISTIC 2

The brand stays relevant.
Brands must stay relevant in the eyes of customers. This relevance is maintained not only by incorporating the latest new features and benefits into given nonprofit offerings but also by taking steps to ensure that the imagery associated with brands accurately reflects modern society.

Brands are image laden. They convey feelings and emotions—aspects of human life that change over time. Given this, nonprofit executives must ensure that they devote significant attention to both the tangible and intangible aspects of branded products in an effort to keep their brands relevant in the eyes of customers.

CHARACTERISTIC 3

The pricing strategy is based on customers' perceptions of value.
Pricing in the nonprofit sector is highly varied. In some cases, customers themselves pay for given goods and services (e.g., a garden club membership, a theater ticket permitting admission, private school tuition); in other cases, third parties pay for products on behalf of eligible clients (e.g., meals prepared for and delivered to underprivileged senior citizens, overnight accommodations for the homeless, dental care for the poverty stricken). Regardless of who ultimately pays for product offerings, nonprofit executives must ensure that product pricing equates with the value delivered by the particular goods and services. In essence, a balance must be struck between the price of the given offerings and associated product features and benefits. The more balanced the relationship, the more likely nonprofit executives can meet the value expectations of customers and associated third parties who provide payment on behalf of designated clients.

CHARACTERISTIC 4

The brand is properly positioned.

As identity vehicles, brands are essential to the practice of product positioning, where nonprofit executives seek to influence customer perceptions of their offerings by determining an appropriate and effective image for products to convey to target audiences. In positioning products, nonprofit executives must determine, for example, whether they have established appropriate points of parity (i.e., areas where products meet the strengths of competitive offerings) and points of difference (i.e., areas where products outperform competitive offerings).

A church-sponsored child day care center, for example, that successfully incorporates these points communicates to customers that it offers all the benefits provided by competing day care centers in addition to value-added features (e.g., better qualified staff members, more convenient hours of operation, a wider array of activities, a more convenient location) that distinguish it from rivals.

Products that are poorly positioned are destined to fail because they do not elicit desired perceptions in the minds of customers. Given this, nonprofit executives must place significant attention on this important marketing aspect.

CHARACTERISTIC 5

The brand is consistent.

One of the most important aspects of branding involves consistency in the presentation of brands in the marketplace. Given the ever-increasing array of advertising media that nonprofit executives have at their disposal, achieving consistency in presentation has become a most challenging task.

If a community college simultaneously portrays itself as "the value leader in higher education" in its radio and television campaigns; "the prestige leader in higher education" in its print and outdoor media campaigns; and "the technology leader in higher education" in its Internet campaign, customers will undoubtedly be confused by the conflicting messages that are being sent.

For given promotional campaigns over given periods of time, it is essential for nonprofit executives to deliver the same consistent message to customers across all advertising media, thus alleviating the confusion associated with multiple conflicting messages.

CHARACTERISTIC 6

The brand portfolio and hierarchy make sense.
The number of brands held by nonprofit organizations varies considerably depending on the characteristics of associated entities. Organizations that offer a limited array of goods and services will likely need only one brand to represent both the given entity and its product offerings. Comprehensive medical centers, universities, technology centers, and other large entities, however, will need to develop multiple brands that accurately represent their many product offerings.

When multiple brands exist, it is very important for nonprofit executives to ensure that their brand portfolios (i.e., the overall collection of brands held by an organization) and brand hierarchies (i.e., the method of organizing brands within a brand portfolio) are appropriate. Importantly, nonprofit executives must ensure that they do not place too many products under one brand name. They also must ensure that they avoid overlapping two brands within the same portfolio.

All brands impact the value of associated brand portfolios. The better organized the brands, the more likely the arrangement will make sense to nonprofit executives and their target audiences. Appropriately arranged hierarchies, in essence, facilitate brand performance.

CHARACTERISTIC 7

The brand makes use of and coordinates a full repertoire of marketing activities to build equity.
Every marketing effort represents an opportunity to increase brand awareness, thus increasing *brand equity*—the value of a brand. Nonprofit executives must be certain to make use of such opportunities by ensuring that brand names, logos, symbols, and the like are prominently featured in advertisements and other promotional campaigns in an effort to facilitate brand awareness. Brands serve as identity vehicles for goods and services. Failure to appropriately incorporate them into associated marketing campaigns is most wasteful.

CHARACTERISTIC 8

The brand's managers understand what the brand means to customers.
Brands have meaning. Some aspects of brands may be viewed positively by customers, while other aspects may be viewed negatively. By understanding exactly what brands mean to customers, nonprofit executives are better prepared to make decisions involving product offerings. Failure to view brands through the eyes of customers can lead to disaster.

For example, a workforce development center that has achieved a reputation for offering helpful, attentive service to job seekers would likely lose a considerable portion of its clientele if it initiated a plan to downsize, reducing the number of staff members available to serve customers. Such a move would undoubtedly increase workloads and reduce the amount of time that job counselors could devote to job seekers, immediately eroding the center's now *former* brand asset of helpful, attentive employment assistance.

Progressive nonprofit executives understand what brands mean to customers. With this understanding, they can make appropriate decisions that build brand equity.

CHARACTERISTIC 9

The brand is given proper support and that support is sustained over the long run.
Building and maintaining brand equity requires a significant and sustained investment. All too often, however, nonprofit entities withdraw funding after initial marketing success, believing that newly established brands have the power to maintain and possibly grow market share without additional resource expenditures. When this withdrawal of funding occurs, however, it opens the door for competitors to take away any previous market share victories.

Whether the retrenchment of resources is in the form of reduced advertising dollars, reduced research and development investments, or even the declining interest of institutional leaders, brand performance will undoubtedly suffer, which dramatically increases the likelihood of product failure. As with any administrative operation, removal of attention, support, and other resources from branding initiatives results in brand decline and, ultimately, failure. Quite obviously, nonprofit executives must work to ensure that appropriate, sustained resources are devoted to brands.

CHARACTERISTIC 10

The organization monitors sources of brand equity.
Prudent brand management requires the ongoing assessment of brand performance in the marketplace. Ideally, nonprofit executives should periodically conduct a *brand equity audit* that includes a *brand inventory* (i.e., an internal compilation identifying all the brands held by an organization along with detailed information outlining how each brand is to be marketed) and a *brand exploratory* (i.e., an external analysis that seeks to discover what brands mean to customers).

If this information is then placed in a *brand equity charter* (i.e., a formal document that identifies and describes brand management fundamentals associated with given product offerings), nonprofit executives are afforded with an invaluable tool that assesses current brand performance and provides guidance for brand management. Without such evaluative instruments, brand equity and its associated sources cannot accurately be assessed.

OPERATIONAL MATTERS

Figure 12-2 illustrates a bar chart that reflects the results of a Brand Report Card completed by a civic club. This diagram clearly depicts the club's brand performance, notably indicating strengths in characteristics 1, 2, 5, and 9 and weaknesses in characteristics 3, 6, and 10. With this information, nonprofit executives can take steps to build upon strengths and reduce or eliminate weaknesses, thus increasing brand performance. Any adjustments, however, should be made cautiously, making sure not to disrupt current strengths.

If desired, nonprofit executives can gain additional insights by completing Brand Report Cards for competing products because they would likely yield useful information regarding rival offerings.

SUMMARY

Through its identification of 10 characteristics possessed by excellent brands, Keller's Brand Report Card provides nonprofit executives with a useful tool for assessing brands. This evaluative device greatly simplifies the activity of monitoring brand performance, providing nonprofit

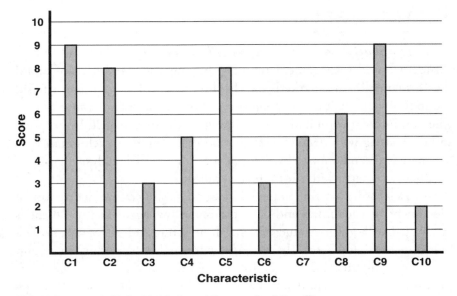

FIGURE 12-2 A Civic Club's Brand Report Card Bar Chart

executives with concise brand assessments that can be used to improve brand management activities and thus increase brand equity.

EXERCISES

1. Provide a detailed overview of Kevin Lane Keller's Brand Report Card, explaining its importance as an evaluative tool for assessing brand performance in the nonprofit sector. Be sure to add into your discussion details regarding the imperative of analyzing brand performance throughout the product life cycle and methods for operationalizing the Brand Report Card accordingly. Based on your knowledge of your local marketplace, do you view area nonprofit entities to be actively engaged in maintaining their brand identities? Why do you believe this to be the case?

2. Contact a local nonprofit entity and arrange an informational interview with its top executive. Present Kevin Lane Keller's Brand Report Card to this executive and request that he or she complete the instrument. On completion of the Brand Report Card, interview

this individual to ascertain the bases for given rankings. Conclude the interview by asking the executive about his or her perceptions regarding the value of the Brand Report Card. Prepare a written narrative of your experiences and findings.

REFERENCE

Keller, K. L. (2000, January/February). The brand report card. *Harvard Business Review, 78*, 147–157.

David Taylor's Brand Stretch Spectrum

INTRODUCTION

On an ongoing basis, nonprofit executives put forward intensive efforts to develop the brands they are responsible for managing. Such concentrated attention to brand management responsibilities is to be expected because of the many benefits that successful brands afford to nonprofit entities. Most notably, brands establish product identity, allowing customers to easily locate the goods and services of given organizations and differentiate them from competitive offerings. When nonprofit executives develop successful brands, they deliver valuable institutional assets that, if well managed, will yield enduring benefits for their associated organizations.

Brand management initiatives are called upon for a variety of reasons, one of which is new product development. When new products are developed, nonprofit executives encounter numerous branding issues, with one of the most notable being the determination of whether new goods and services will carry existing brand names, termed *brand extensions*, or be assigned entirely new ones.

Whether to field brand extensions or introduce new brands requires careful consideration. Brand extensions carry the benefit of familiarity in that target audiences already possess an awareness of associated brand names. This familiarity certainly affords advantages for new offerings in that the burden of building a base identity is significantly reduced and might even be outright eliminated depending on the strength of established brand names.

Despite this powerful benefit, brand extensions are not always desirable. Brand portfolios can occasionally be overextended with too many products carrying given badges, resulting in confusion for both nonprofit executives and their customer populations. New product offerings also might not logically fit under existing brand names, warranting that such offerings carry newly developed identities.

Significantly, brand extensions carry risks associated with the application of successful brand names to new and unproven product offerings. If these new products are not successful, such offerings will likely diminish the overall value of the brand names that they carry, negatively impacting all the other product offerings in the brand portfolio. Regardless, the extension of established brand names to newly developed product offerings represents a practice worthy of consideration any time new goods and services present themselves.

Interestingly, in the course of managing brands, nonprofit executives may discover logical additions to existing product arrays, resulting in various brand extensions. Hence, brand extensions can spur new product development even in the absence of formal initiatives to do so.

For assistance whenever brand extensions are under consideration, nonprofit executives can turn to the Brand Stretch Spectrum, a tool developed by David Taylor. Illustrated in Figure 13-1, Taylor's Brand Stretch Spectrum identifies three paths for extending, or stretching, existing brands: the core range extension, the direct stretch extension, and the indirect stretch extension.

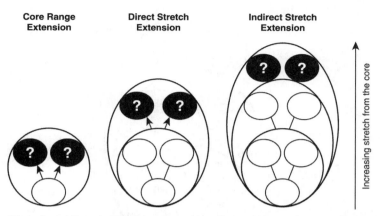

Core Range Extension   **Direct Stretch Extension**   **Indirect Stretch Extension**

Increasing stretch from the core

Adapted from Brand Stretch: Why 1 in 2 Extensions Fail and How to Beat the Odds by David Taylor. Copyright © 2004 by John Wiley & Sons Limited.

FIGURE 13-1 Taylor's Brand Stretch Spectrum

Each of these paths presents opportunities for growth and expansion under the right circumstances, with risk increasing as extensions move further away from core product offerings. These three brand extension pathways, accompanied by examples in Figures 13-2 and 13-3, are explained as follows.

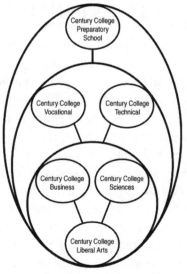

Constructed using design methodologies in Taylor, David. 2004. Brand stretch: Why 1 in 2 extensions fail and how to beat the odds. Chichester, West Sussex, UK: Wiley.

FIGURE 13-2 A College's Brand Stretch Spectrum

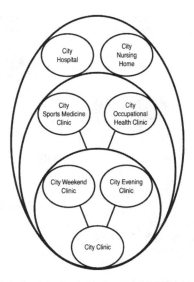

Constructed using design methodologies in Taylor, David. 2004. Brand stretch: Why 1 in 2 extensions fail and how to beat the odds. Chichester, West Sussex, UK: Wiley.

FIGURE 13-3 A Medical Clinic's Brand Stretch Spectrum

THE CORE RANGE EXTENSION

The core range extension represents the application of a brand name to a new version (i.e., a product-form variant) of an existing branded product. Because the brand is applied to a product with common core characteristics, such extensions are quite logical and reasonably safe pursuits.

A college that introduces a business school and a sciences school to complement its existing liberal arts school, for example, would represent a core range extension. So too would a newly established weekend medical clinic that carried the brand name of an existing weekday clinic.

Core range extensions are essentially equivalent product offerings, distinguished only by moderate feature and benefit differences. With such products, brand extensions make perfect sense because the given offerings are so closely related to each other. This similarity affords excellent opportunities for newly developed goods and services to benefit from existing brand awareness in the marketplace.

THE DIRECT STRETCH EXTENSION

The direct stretch extension involves the application of an existing brand name to a broadened array of goods and services that differs from the core offering upon which the extension was based. This extension essentially stretches the brand name to cover items within a particular product class that extend beyond the specific product from which the brand name was derived.

An example of a direct stretch extension would be a college that offers traditional academic degree programs and decides to introduce vocational and technical education programs under its existing brand name. Another example would be a clinic that offers primary care services placing a new specialty care clinic under its existing brand name.

Although direct stretch extensions differ from the core offerings that provided their associated brand identities, these extensions do fit into like product classes. Regardless, direct stretch extensions carry a greater degree of risk than core range extensions because the associated product offerings are different. This risk necessitates that nonprofit executives carefully evaluate direct stretch initiatives to ensure that these extensions represent appropriate applications for existing brand names.

THE INDIRECT STRETCH EXTENSION

The indirect stretch extension involves entry into a new product class. The degree of differentiation between the existing product class and the newly pursued one can range from mild to substantial. Because indirect stretch extensions branch out into unrelated product classes, they stretch brand names across a wide array of diverse product offerings, essentially creating umbrella brands.

A college exclusively focused on the higher education product class would effect an indirect stretch extension by introducing a college preparatory school under the brand name carried by its higher education offerings. A medical clinic focused on the provision of comprehensive medical services in outpatient settings would effect an indirect stretch extension if the establishment decided to construct and operate a hospital or nursing home.

Indirect stretch extensions pierce through the current product classes pursued by nonprofit entities, placing them in new product classes containing goods and services that may or may not be closely associated with the goods and services offered in existing product classes. Clearly, indirect stretch extensions carry the highest level of risk associated with stretching brand names because established identities are being applied to product classes that are new and different. Given this, nonprofit executives must ensure that a good fit exists between new product classes and existing brand identities because weak connections might diminish existing brand equity.

OPERATIONAL MATTERS

Taylor's Brand Stretch Spectrum identifies three potential paths for extending brand names to cover products that are increasingly distant from the core offerings upon which the brand names originated. Each of these extensions can be successfully effected under the right circumstances.

As with any new product pursuit, extensions should carefully be evaluated to ensure that markets for given products exist and that the application of existing brand names to new offerings makes sense to both internal and external audiences. If these conditions are met, the brand extension route affords many opportunities for marketing success. If, however, new goods and services appear to possess great potential, but existing brand names do not seem to represent appropriate identities for these new offerings, the establishment of entirely new brand identities would likely yield better marketing results.

Significantly, Taylor's Brand Stretch Spectrum can be used to spark new product ideas. By understanding the various pathways for stretching brands, nonprofit executives can review their existing product arrays and ask themselves how they might go about effecting core range, direct stretch, and indirect stretch extensions. This activity can yield very productive new product insights even if formal systems for new product development do not exist. It is not uncommon for some of the best new product ideas to grow out of existing product offerings and, when this happens, the application of existing brand names to these new goods and services offers excellent opportunities to quickly connect with target audiences.

SUMMARY

David Taylor's Brand Stretch Spectrum provides nonprofit executives with a useful portrayal of potential paths for effecting brand extensions. Aside from its use as a tool for understanding such extensions, Taylor's Brand Stretch Spectrum can be used to foster new product development initiatives by encouraging nonprofit executives to envision how they might potentially extend their product arrays beyond core offerings.

EXERCISES

1. Define and comprehensively discuss David Taylor's Brand Stretch Spectrum, providing insights into its guidance and use as a device for the extension of core brands. Preface your discussion by reflecting on the advantages and disadvantages associated with brand extensions. How would you characterize the prevalence of brand extensions in the nonprofit sector? What is the basis of your characterization?

2. Select a nonprofit good or service of your choice and assign the product an appropriate brand name. Using David Taylor's Brand Stretch Spectrum, envision potential brand extensions to this hypothetical offering by formulating core range extensions, direct stretch extensions, and indirect stretch extensions. Provide an illustration of your Brand Stretch Spectrum and offer a narrative explaining your rationale for assembling the brand portfolio as you did.

REFERENCE

Taylor, D. (2004). *Brand stretch: Why 1 in 2 extensions fail and how to beat the odds.* Chichester, U.K.: Wiley.

PART III

Target Marketing Tools

CHAPTER 14

The Market-Product Grid

LEARNING OBJECTIVES

After examining this chapter, readers will have the ability to:

- Understand the three-step process of target marketing and its importance in the nonprofit sector.
- Realize the benefits afforded to nonprofit organizations as a result of target marketing practices.
- Understand major segmentation variables upon which markets can be divided.
- Recognize the value of the Market-Product Grid as an instrument for segmenting markets and targeting appropriate segments.

INTRODUCTION

Target marketing is often employed in order to more effectively address the wants and needs of customers. Target marketing involves three interrelated activities: market segmentation, targeting, and product positioning. Market segmentation is the process of dividing a market into groups (i.e., segments) of individuals who share common characteristics. When the market has been segmented, targeting ensues. Targeting involves the selection of attractive segments on which establishments will focus their efforts, working to satisfy the wants and needs of these groups. These targeted segments are known as an entity's target market. Product positioning follows targeting and

involves the determination of an appropriate and effective image for products to convey to customers.

Target marketing developed out of the desire to more appropriately
address the various wants and needs of different customer groups. The
practice stands in contrast to mass marketing, which involves offering
products to the market as a whole, without regard for individual tastes
and preferences.

Target marketing makes sense. For example, low-income earners have
needs for entitlement programs that are of little concern to those with
greater resources. Parents with young children, unlike those with older
children or none at all, have needs for educational offerings through kin-
dergartens and elementary schools. Senior citizens have needs for support
services that are unnecessary for younger members of the population.

By focusing on the specific wants and needs of market segments,
nonprofit executives can deliver goods and services that are specifically
tailored to the associated groups. This practice not only improves customer satisfaction but also allows for better use of promotions resources
through the selection of communications vehicles that precisely reach
desired populations.

A useful tool for target marketing is known as the Market-Product
Grid, an instrument that specifically addresses the segmenting and targeting aspects of marketing. Illustrated in Figure 14-1, the Market-Product
Grid, as depicted by Roger Kerin, Eric Berkowitz, Steven Hartley, and
William Rudelius, consists of a matrix with markets identified on its vertical axis and products identified on its horizontal axis. The actual number
of cells in the matrix is, of course, dependent on the number of markets
and products identified. As a result, Market-Product Grids range from
being quite small for entities with few markets and few products to
being very large for entities that offer multiple markets an extensive array
of products.

To create a Market-Product Grid, nonprofit executives simply
(1) construct a matrix of sufficient size, (2) list potential markets on the vertical axis, (3) list product offerings on the horizontal axis, and (4) evaluate
each of the resulting market-product combinations, characterizing them as
large, medium, small, or nonexistent markets.

Products Markets	Product 1	Product 2	Product 3
Market 1	?	?	?
Market 2	?	?	?
Market 3	?	?	?

3 = Large Market, 2 = Medium Market, 1 = Small Market, 0 = No Market

Adapted from Marketing, 7th ed. by Roger A. Kerin, Eric N. Berkowitz, Steven W. Hartley, and William Rudelius. Copyright © 2003, 2000, 1997, 1994, 1992, 1989, 1986 by The McGraw-Hill Companies, Inc. Published by McGraw-Hill. Reproduced with permission of The McGraw-Hill Companies, Inc.

FIGURE 14-1 The Market-Product Grid

The activity of listing the goods and services of establishments on the Market-Product Grid is quite simple, but identifying and listing potential markets can be somewhat challenging without some point of reference. This point of reference can often be found by consulting a breakdown of segmentation variables, such as the one listed in Table 14-1.

This table provides examples of specific segments that exist within each of the four major segmentation categories: geographic, demographic, psychographic, and behavioral. However, it presents only a few of the almost endless market segments that nonprofit executives could potentially pursue. Such a table serves as a useful starting point for identifying markets for placement on the Market-Product Grid.

Table 14-1 Major Segmentation Variables

Geographic

World region / country	North America, Western Europe, Middle East, Pacific Rim, China, India, Canada, Mexico
Country region	Pacific, Mountain, West North Central, West South Central, East North Central, East South Central, South Atlantic, Middle Atlantic, New England
City or metro size	Under 5,000; 5,000–20,000; 20,000–50,000; 50,000–100,000; 100,000–250,000; 250,000–500,000; 500,000–1,000,000; 1,000,000–4,000,000; 4,000,000+
Density	Urban, suburban, rural
Climate	Northern, southern

Demographic

Age	Under 6, 6–11, 12–19, 20–34, 35–49, 50–64, 65+
Gender	Male, female
Family size	1–2, 3–4, 5+
Family life cycle	Young, single; young, married, no children; young, married with children; older, married with children; older, married, no children under 18; older, single; other
Income	Under $10,000; $10,000–$20,000; $20,000–$30,000; $30,000–$50,000; $50,000–$100,000; $100,000+
Occupation	Professional and technical; managers, officials, and proprietors; clerical; sales; craftspeople; supervisors; operatives; farmers; retired; students; homemakers; unemployed
Education	Grade school or less, some high school, high school graduate, some college, college graduate
Religion	Catholic, Protestant, Jewish, Muslim, Hindu, other
Race	Asian, Hispanic, black, white
Generation	Baby boomer, Generation X, Generation Y
Nationality	North American, South American, British, French, German, Italian, Japanese

Psychographic

Social class	Lower lowers, upper lowers, working class, middle class, upper middles, lower uppers, upper uppers
Lifestyle	Achievers, strivers, strugglers
Personality	Compulsive, gregarious, authoritarian, ambitious

Behavioral

Occasions	Regular occasion, special occasion
Benefits	Quality, service, economy, convenience, speed
User status	Nonuser, ex-user, potential user, first-time user, regular user
User rates	Light user, medium user, heavy user
Loyalty status	None, medium, strong, absolute

Table 14-1 Major Segmentation Variables (*Continued*)

Readiness stage	Unaware, aware, informed, interested, desirous, intending to buy
Attitude toward product	Enthusiastic, positive, indifferent, negative, hostile

Source: Kotler, P., & Armstrong, G. (2004). *Principles of Marketing* (10th ed.). Upper Saddle River, NJ: Prentice Hall. Adapted by permission of Pearson Education, Inc., Upper Saddle River, NJ. Reprinted by permission.

OPERATIONAL MATTERS

Figure 14-2 illustrates a Market-Product Grid that was developed for a meal delivery charity. Here, the charity used the grid to assess the market potential of different areas of Jackson County. The grid indicates that the south and central sections of Jackson County possess large markets, the east section possesses a medium market, and the north and

Products Markets	Meal Delivery Service
North	1
South	3
East	2
West	1
Central	3

(Jackson County)

3 = Large Market, 2 = Medium Market, 1 = Small Market, 0 = No Market

Constructed using design methodologies in Kerin, Roger A., Eric N. Berkowitz, Steven W. Hartley, and William Rudelius. Marketing. 7th ed. New York: McGraw-Hill, 2003.

FIGURE 14-2 A Meal Delivery Charity's Market-Product Grid

west sections contain small markets. The grid clearly identifies the most prominent markets (i.e., the south and central regions) for the charity's meal program within the county—information that can greatly assist the organization in determining how it goes about addressing the targeted population. Such information might, for example, help the charity determine where to locate satellite offices, how to schedule transportation to and from various residences, and so on.

Figure 14-3 presents a more complex Market-Product Grid that was developed for a community theater. Here, the theater sought to examine Washington County's market potential for various theatrical productions by genre. The grid notably reveals a prominent market across all genres for young adults. Other age groups are mixed regarding their attraction to various genres, with preferences being centered on particular types of productions. The horror genre appears to be very limited. Such details shed significant light on segment opportunities, giving the theater insights into what particular productions it should seek to offer in the community.

It should be noted that although the largest markets might seem to represent the most productive marketing pursuits, such markets are not always appropriate targets. For example, nonprofit entities must factor in

Markets / Products	Community Theater Productions					
	Comedy	Mystery	Drama	Action	Romance	Horror
Young Children	1	0	0	1	0	0
Teenagers	3	1	1	3	2	3
Young Adults	3	2	3	2	3	2
Middle-Aged Adults	1	2	2	1	2	0
Senior Citizens	1	3	2	0	1	0

(Washington County)

3 = Large Market, 2 = Medium Market, 1 = Small Market, 0 = No Market

Constructed using design methodologies in Kerin, Roger A., Eric N. Berkowitz, Steven W. Hartley, and William Rudelius. Marketing. 7th ed. New York: McGraw-Hill, 2003.

FIGURE 14-3 A Community Theater's Market-Product Grid

marketplace competitors, their dominance in certain segments, and their overall numbers. Certain segments, although large, may be saturated with competitors or dominated by market leaders. In such situations, smaller markets with fewer competitors may be more desirable segments to pursue. Aside from competitive elements, nonprofit organizations might select smaller markets based on the particular missions they embrace. Those entities that cater to underserved, rural populations represent excellent examples of nonprofit institutions engaging in this practice.

It should also be noted that Market-Product Grids are only as accurate as the information that is used to complete them. Although they remain useful even with informally collected data, the use of data derived from formal market research can greatly improve their accuracy.

SUMMARY

The Market-Product Grid provides a simple, yet highly useful, method for segmenting and targeting markets. By using this tool, nonprofit executives can more precisely identify and target appropriate customer groups. The Market-Product Grid also ensures that nonprofit executives consider multiple market opportunities.

EXERCISES

1. Define and comprehensively discuss the Market-Product Grid and its role as an instrument for segmenting markets and targeting appropriate segments. Preface your discussion by sharing insights regarding the value of target marketing in the nonprofit sector.

2. Visit the website of an area nonprofit entity and identify as many of its product offerings as possible. Based on your knowledge of your local region, identify potential markets for these products. With this information, construct a Market-Product Grid for the given nonprofit organization, being sure to evaluate the resulting market-product combinations. Then, prepare a narrative describing the most appropriate targets based on your analysis. Are the targets you selected consistent with the perceived selections of the given nonprofit entity? Explain your rationale.

REFERENCES

Kerin, R. A., Berkowitz, E. N., Hartley, S. W., & Rudelius, W. (2003). *Marketing* (7th ed.). New York, NY: McGraw-Hill.

Kotler, P., & Armstrong, G. (2004). *Principles of marketing* (10th ed.). Upper Saddle River, NJ: Prentice Hall.

CHAPTER 15

Kotler and Trias de Bes' Lateral Marketing Strategy

LEARNING OBJECTIVES

After examining this chapter, readers will have the ability to:

- Appreciate the value of target marketing as an important nonprofit marketing activity.
- Understand the practice of vertical segmentation, the traditional approach to market segmentation, which involves identifying viable segments by drilling down into markets.
- Understand the practice of lateral segmentation, a nontraditional approach to market segmentation, which encourages nonprofit executives to look broadly at markets to identify previously overlooked opportunities.
- Appreciate the value of Kotler and Trias de Bes' Lateral Marketing Strategy as an instrument for realizing the true depth and breadth of marketplace opportunities when it is used in tandem with traditional approaches.

INTRODUCTION

Target marketing—the three interrelated activities of market segmentation, targeting, and product positioning—represents one of the most important marketing practices. This practice essentially tailors products

113

for specific market segments in an effort to encourage exchange. Clearly more productive than mass marketing, which involves marketing goods and services to broad markets without regard for individual tastes and preferences, target marketing places a defined emphasis on serving specific customer populations and represents a very common marketing practice.

Despite the obvious benefits that the practice of target marketing affords to nonprofit executives and their customers, there are refinements that can improve the practice. One area of improvement concerns the first step of target marketing: market segmentation.

Specifically, market segmentation is the process of dividing a market into groups (i.e., segments) of individuals who share common characteristics. Market segmentation is typically effected by drilling down into markets, bypassing layers that are deemed undesirable until desirable layers of associated markets have been identified. Appealing market segments are then targeted. This very common, drill-down orientation of market segmentation can be termed *vertical segmentation.*

Vertical segmentation is clearly a viable method for segmenting markets, but as illustrated in Figure 15-1, the practice of drilling down

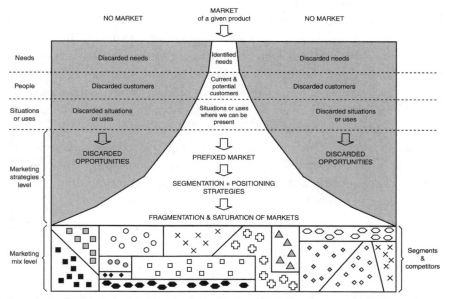

From Lateral Marketing: New Techniques for Finding Breakthrough Ideas by Philip Kotler and Fernando Trias de Bes. Copyright © 2003 by Philip Kotler and Fernando Trias de Bes. Reprinted with permission of John Wiley & Sons, Inc.

FIGURE 15-1 Vertical Segmentation & Missed Opportunities

into markets results in many missed opportunities. Such opportunities, although historically passed up, offer rich growth possibilities worthy of exploration. To aid organizations in improving their segmentation results by identifying missed opportunities, Philip Kotler and Fernando Trias de Bes formulated the Lateral Marketing Strategy, a method for introducing *lateral segmentation* into the array of traditional segmentation tools.

Kotler and Trias de Bes developed the Lateral Marketing Strategy to encourage entities to look broadly at their markets in an attempt to identify opportunities to serve customer groups that had previously been overlooked, courtesy of the drill-down orientation of vertical marketing. The technique is beneficial in that it permits the identification of new segments to pursue. Significantly, it also benefits customers whose wants and needs might otherwise go unnoticed.

THE LATERAL MARKETING STRATEGY APPROACH

Lateral Marketing Strategy essentially requires that nonprofit executives carefully examine their served market segments and the products that are used to address those segments. Specifically, they must endeavor to determine what market segment opportunities, if any, have been overlooked or bypassed over the course of serving current customer populations. Previously forgone segments are then evaluated to determine whether they are worthy of pursuit, with noted segments becoming potential target markets.

Consider a church that has, as part of its product array, constructed a family life center to serve its congregation. The family life center clearly provides benefits for its target market—the members of the church—but what potential opportunities have been overlooked? Depending on the capacity of the family life center, opportunities for it to also serve as a resource for other populations, in keeping with its mission, might exist. Perhaps the center could play a role in hosting afterschool programs for disadvantaged youths. Perhaps the center could provide shelter for the homeless population during inclement weather. As this example demonstrates, lateral segmentation initiatives require a degree of exploration and creativity on the part of nonprofit executives, but they afford a range of segmentation opportunities that might otherwise be neglected.

Importantly, Kotler and Trias de Bes note that lateral segmentation is not a substitute for vertical segmentation. Instead, it is a complementary technique that increases the potential for the identification of market segments. When vertical and lateral segmentation approaches are combined, nonprofit executives significantly increase the range of growth opportunities at their disposal.

SUMMARY

Kotler and Trias de Bes' Lateral Marketing Strategy provides nonprofit executives with an innovative method for broadly viewing segment opportunities in the marketplace. By adding lateral segmentation to their existing array of segmentation tools, nonprofit executives better position themselves and their organizations for enduring marketing success.

EXERCISES

1. Define and discuss vertical-segmentation and lateral-segmentation techniques and provide details regarding their respective deployment in the nonprofit sector. Do you view Kotler and Trias de Bes' Lateral Marketing Strategy as a technique that will compel nonprofit entities to reevaluate their segmentation practices? Explain your rationale.
2. Reflect on the various nonprofit organizations in your local community and their respective targets. Can you identify any attractive opportunities that were possibly overlooked? If so, what are they?

REFERENCE

Kotler, P., & Trias de Bes, F. (2003). *Lateral marketing: New techniques for finding breakthrough ideas*. Hoboken, NJ: Wiley.

CHAPTER 16

Philip Kotler's Segment-by-Segment Invasion Plan

LEARNING OBJECTIVES

After examining this chapter, readers will have the ability to:

- Understand that all market segments, if successfully pursued, will eventually be exhausted of growth opportunities.
- Realize the imperative of identifying not only those market segments to pursue in the present but also those segments that will be pursued in the future.
- Appreciate the value and utility afforded by Philip Kotler's Segment-by-Segment Invasion Plan as a tool for mapping current and future market segment pursuits.

INTRODUCTION

When progressive nonprofit executives engage in target marketing, they not only identify the market segments they wish to immediately pursue but also the market segments they might target in the future. In essence, they formulate plans that outline current and future market segment pursuits. This practice is beneficial because all market segments, if successfully pursued, will eventually be exhausted of growth opportunities for given product offerings. By proactively identifying future market

117

segments to pursue, nonprofit executives are better prepared to embark on a course of sustained growth.

The practice of identifying future market segment pursuits is greatly facilitated through the use of Philip Kotler's Segment-by-Segment Invasion Plan. As illustrated in Figure 16-1, the Invasion Plan consists of a vertical axis, representing product varieties, and a horizontal axis, representing customer groups. Each of the resulting cells in the matrix identifies market segments that are available to pursue, with the actual number of cells being dependent, of course, on the number of product varieties and customer groups identified.

To create an Invasion Plan, nonprofit executives (1) construct a matrix of sufficient size; (2) list product varieties on the vertical axis; (3) list customer groups on the horizontal axis; (4) identify, using unique hatch patterns, all the organizations that are currently pursuing the market segments formed in the matrix; and (5) identify, using arrows, the market segments that represent desirable future pursuits for the evaluating entity.

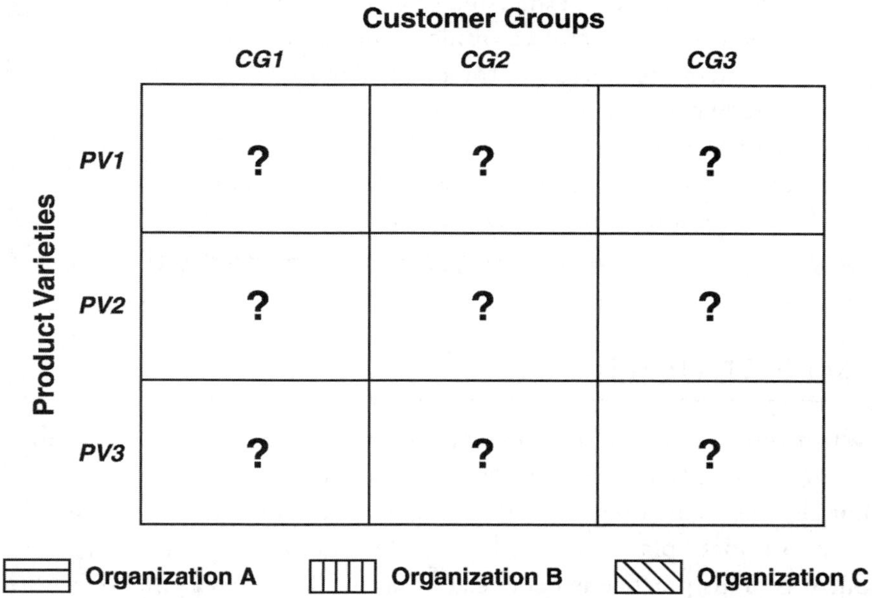

From Kotler, Philip, Marketing Management, 11th Edition, © 2003. Adapted by permission of Pearson Education, Inc., Upper Saddle River, NJ. Reprinted with permission.

FIGURE 16-1 Kotler's Segment-by-Segment Invasion Plan

The resulting Segment-by-Segment Invasion Plan provides nonprofit executives with a concise assessment of current market segment pursuits. It also illustrates the anticipated future market segment pursuits of the evaluating organization.

OPERATIONAL MATTERS

Figure 16-2 illustrates a Segment-by-Segment Invasion Plan that was developed for Madison Wellness, a physical therapy clinic. The diagram indicates that Madison Wellness is targeting the adult and senior markets for physical therapy services; Oakdale Clinic is targeting the youth market for speech therapy services; and Village Therapies is targeting the youth, adult, and senior markets for speech therapy services.

Seeking increased growth, Madison Wellness is planning to expand beyond its current physical therapy offering by first entering the occupational therapy market, targeting adults and seniors simultaneously, as indicated by the first series of arrows in the illustration. If successful, Madison Wellness will later enter the speech therapy market, once again

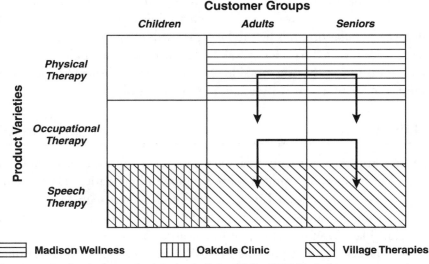

Constructed using design methodologies in Kotler, Philip. 2003. Marketing management. 11th ed. Upper Saddle River, NJ: Prentice Hall.

FIGURE 16-2 A Physical Therapy Clinic's Invasion Plan

targeting both adults and seniors, as indicated by the second series of arrows in the illustration. With this information, Madison Wellness has a concise portrayal of the current market segment pursuits of identified competitors. The clinic also possesses a useful depiction of the market segments that it might pursue in the future.

Beyond the depiction of current and future market segment pursuits, Kotler's Segment-by-Segment Invasion Plan affords nonprofit executives with opportunities to formulate marketing strategies and tactics associated with their growth pursuits. They can, for example, assess barriers to entry, evaluate competitors, predict competitive responses to invasions, and assess segment limitations. Proactively addressing the requirements of upcoming segment invasions increases the likelihood that pursuits will be successful.

It should be noted that nonprofit executives must ensure that their Segment-by-Segment Invasion Plans are kept strictly confidential; something that is all the more essential for those entities that are engaged in intensive marketplace competition with myriad organizations offering similar products. If competitors gain access to such information, the element of surprise is, of course, eliminated. Competitors will then have the opportunity to take preemptive actions against anticipated segment invasions, making invasions much more difficult or even impossible.

Even for those nonprofit organizations serving as providers of last resort for given populations, it is best to keep planned invasions confidential until they are revealed to the outside world through their implementation. Such measures reduce the outside chance of being upstaged by another nonprofit entity seeking to capitalize on the ideas of others.

SUMMARY

Despite success in particular market segments, nonprofit executives must understand that every segment possesses growth boundaries. Therefore, if sustained growth is desired, new markets and market segments must be identified and pursued—a task facilitated by Kotler's Segment-by-Segment Invasion Plan. Usefully, this tool forces nonprofit executives to identify future market segment pursuits that will yield sustained organizational performance.

EXERCISES

1. Provide a detailed account profiling Philip Kotler's Segment-by-Segment Invasion Plan, identifying and explaining its uses and steps of development, accompanied by an appropriate illustration. Share your thoughts on the degree to which nonprofit organizations focus on future market segment pursuits.
2. Contact a local nonprofit entity and arrange an informational interview with its top executive to learn about the organization's segmentation planning practices. Specifically, investigate the degree to which the establishment has defined future segments for pursuit. Present Philip Kotler's Segment-by-Segment Invasion Plan and ask the executive for insights regarding the value of the tool for use in his or her particular workplace. Report your findings in detail.

REFERENCE

Kotler, P. (2003). *Marketing management* (11th ed.). Upper Saddle River, NJ: Prentice Hall.

The Perceptual Map

INTRODUCTION

Target marketing is an essential practice involving three interrelated activities: market segmentation, targeting, and product positioning. Market segmentation is the process of dividing a market into groups (i.e., segments) of individuals who share common characteristics. When the market has been segmented, nonprofit executives engage in targeting, where they select attractive segments and focus their efforts on satisfying the wants and needs of these groups. After completing the segmenting and targeting activities, nonprofit executives position their products accordingly.

Product positioning involves the determination of an appropriate and effective image for products to convey to customers. A credit counseling agency, for example, might wish to portray itself as an establishment that delivers quick results, while another might emphasize its all-encompassing service. A medical clinic might wish to emphasize its prestigious medical staff, while another might convey its convenient service. An astronomical society might wish to convey an image of technological innovation for scientists, while another might desire an image of wholesome entertainment for the entire family. When the ideal image has been determined, nonprofit executives formulate methods to convey the desired product imagery to target markets through advertising, personal selling, sales promotion, and other means.

When products have been positioned, nonprofit executives must monitor consumer perceptions related to the offerings to ensure that associated goods and services are perceived in the manner desired. A useful tool that provides guidance to nonprofit executives in this endeavor is known as the Perceptual (or Positioning) Map, which, as illustrated in Figure 17-1, consists of two

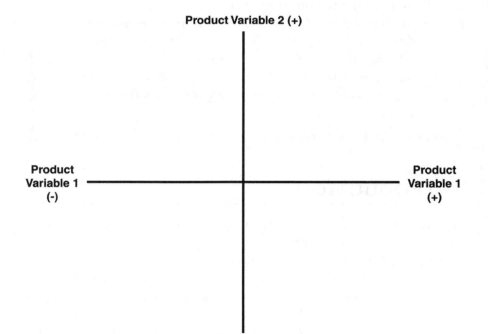

FIGURE 17-1 The Perceptual Map

intersected axes that represent different product-related attributes. When completed, a Perceptual Map demonstrates how consumers perceive products based on designated product attributes—information that is essential for the purpose of product positioning.

To assess products using the Perceptual Map, nonprofit executives (1) identify the offerings to be evaluated, (2) construct the map diagram, as illustrated in Figure 17-1, (3) determine the product-related attributes that will compose the map's axes, labeling the diagram accordingly, (4) gather data pertaining to the consumer perceptions of products to be evaluated, and (5) plot the coordinates of each product on the Perceptual Map. This visual representation is then analyzed to determine if product offerings are perceived in the manner desired, allowing nonprofit executives to make adjustments as necessary. For increased insights into consumer perceptions, nonprofit executives can add competitive products to the Perceptual Map.

OPERATIONAL MATTERS

Figure 17-2 illustrates a Perceptual Map that was completed by a college preparatory school. Here, the school sought to evaluate consumer perceptions regarding its educational offerings in relation to competitive offerings on the basis of expense and prestige. The diagram indicates that two schools—including the evaluating school—are perceived to be more prestigious and more expensive, three schools are perceived to be less prestigious and more expensive, four schools are perceived to be less prestigious and less expensive, and one school is perceived to be more prestigious and less expensive. Of course, by examining each quadrant, more-specific information can be obtained. The evaluating school is, for example, viewed as the most expensive of the two schools in the "more prestigious, more expensive" quadrant, but it is the least prestigious of the two.

With the information provided by the Perceptual Map, the school can take steps to improve the manner in which it is perceived. Because the school was viewed to be less prestigious than two of its competitors, it might consider introducing measures to increase prestige, such as enhanced facilities and better-qualified faculty members. Of course, the school could gain even greater insights by completing additional Perceptual Maps to view consumer perceptions regarding other product attributes.

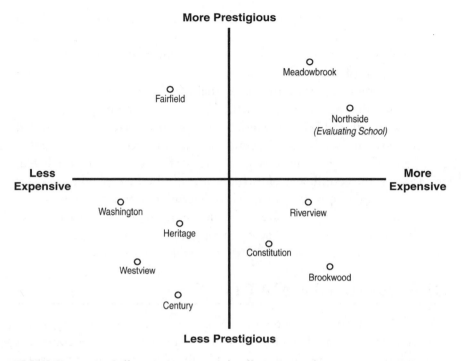

FIGURE 17-2 A College Preparatory School's Perceptual Map

EXPLORATORY PERCEPTUAL MAPS

Beyond assessing current products, Perceptual Maps are also useful for positioning new and anticipated product offerings. Figure 17-3 identifies an Exploratory Perceptual Map that was completed by a drug and alcohol rehabilitation group seeking to assess expansion opportunities in a particular community. Here, the evaluating entity assessed the community's existing rehabilitation centers based on amenities and price. The completed Exploratory Perceptual Map indicates that three rehabilitation centers are perceived to offer many amenities at a high price, one center is perceived to offer few amenities at a low price, and one center is perceived to offer few amenities at a high price.

With this map, the evaluating entity has an enhanced perspective of the drug and alcohol rehabilitation services market in the community, which can guide it in determining how it might possibly enter the market.

FIGURE 17-3 A Drug & Alcohol Rehab Group's Exploratory Perceptual Map

Notably, the diagram illustrates that a void exists in the market's "many amenities, low price" quadrant. This void may represent an opportunity for the evaluating establishment to differentiate itself from existing competitors by establishing the community's only rehabilitation center that offers many amenities at a low price. The Exploratory Perceptual Map also allows the evaluating establishment to assess various competitive approaches to drug and alcohol rehabilitation.

OTHER POINTS

It is important to remember that Perceptual Maps are only as accurate as the information that is used to complete them. In constructing these maps, some nonprofit executives simply use their own judgment regarding consumer perceptions related to the product offerings under examination. Others assemble groups consisting of members of their leadership teams to discuss likely consumer perceptions, developing

Perceptual Maps accordingly. Still other nonprofit executives use formal market research to construct these maps. Although Perceptual Maps remain useful even with informally collected data, the use of data derived from formal market research can greatly improve their accuracy.

It is also important to remember that Perceptual Maps do indeed deal with perceptions. Consumer perceptions, of course, change over time—a fact which necessitates that nonprofit executives routinely construct and analyze Perceptual Maps in an effort to stay abreast of the latest consumer perceptions regarding product offerings.

SUMMARY

The Perceptual Map provides nonprofit executives with a helpful tool for understanding consumer perceptions related to product offerings. The Perceptual Map can be employed to assess consumer perceptions related to both current and anticipated product offerings. Such information greatly assists nonprofit executives in their ongoing product positioning responsibilities, making the Perceptual Map an indispensable marketing tool.

EXERCISES

1. Provide a comprehensive overview of the Perceptual Map, explaining its purpose, components, uses, and benefits, accompanied by an associated illustration. Be sure to indicate how the instrument can be used not only for current product offerings but also for potential product offerings in the marketplace. Share your views regarding how this instrument can be used to effect better product positioning outcomes in the nonprofit sector.

2. Select a nonprofit product of your choice for placement in your local market and envision its key features and benefits. Then, prepare an Exploratory Perceptual Map for the potential offering, selecting applicable product-related attributes for the axes and plotting all competitive products in the market on the diagram based on your views of how consumers might perceive the offerings. Provide a narrative assessing this new product offering in the context of existing competition.

CHAPTER 18

Ries and Trout's Product Ladder

LEARNING OBJECTIVES

After examining this chapter, readers will have the ability to:

- Realize that nonprofit executives must direct attention to the manner in which consumers perceive their product offerings relative to those of competitors.
- Understand that significant efforts are required to ensure that consumers view given nonprofit products more favorably than competitive offerings.
- Recognize that consumers tend to rank products in their minds.
- Appreciate the value of Ries and Trout's Product Ladder as a tool for visualizing and understanding the product rankings formulated by consumers.

INTRODUCTION

Given that nonprofit executives ultimately seek to effect exchanges with target markets, they must constantly focus on the manner in which consumers perceive their products in relation to competitive offerings. Ideally, nonprofit executives would like for consumers to view their goods and services more favorably than those of their competitors. Achieving such prominent positions in the minds of consumers is a difficult task, but if attained, it yields significant benefits.

For insights into attaining such lofty positions in the minds of consumers, nonprofit executives frequently refer to the Product Ladder, a useful tool developed by Al Ries and Jack Trout. Illustrated in Figure 18-1, the Product Ladder consists of an outline of a human head, representing a consumer's mind, with a ladder situated inside, representing the consumer's rank order of brands within a particular product category.

Ries and Trout developed the Product Ladder to illustrate that, given the limitations of the human mind coupled with the proliferation of available goods and services in the marketplace, consumers are forced to rank products in their minds. These rankings can be depicted as a series of ladders in the minds of consumers, with each ladder representing a different product category and each step representing a different product brand. Products situated on higher steps rank higher in the minds of consumers than products situated on lower steps.

Product Ladders may consist of one step or many steps, although Product Ladders with seven or more steps are considered to be quite lengthy. Product

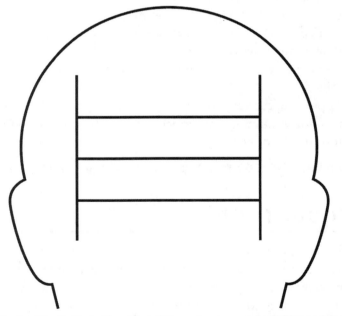

From Positioning: The Battle for Your Mind, 20th anniversary ed. by Al Ries and Jack Trout. Copyright © 2001, 1981 by The McGraw-Hill Companies, Inc. Published by McGraw-Hill. Reproduced with permission of The McGraw-Hill Companies, Inc.

FIGURE 18-1 Ries & Trout's Product Ladder

Ladders are also consumer specific—they are based on the particular views of given individuals.

Some consumers may not be aware of brands within particular product categories and would, therefore, not possess associated Product Ladders. Consumers who, for example, have never had a need for graduate education may not possess a Product Ladder for graduate degree programs. When consumers develop needs for unfamiliar goods and services, however, Product Ladders form rather quickly as consumers actively solicit information regarding given product offerings through both formal and informal channels.

OPERATIONAL MATTERS

To assess products using the Product Ladder, nonprofit executives simply (1) identify the product category to be evaluated, (2) gather data pertaining to the consumer perceptions of product brands within the identified category, and (3) construct a Product Ladder that is representative of the findings. This visual representation is then analyzed to gain product insights.

Figure 18-2 presents a series of Product Ladders illustrating a particular consumer's perceptions regarding a variety of nonprofit offerings; namely,

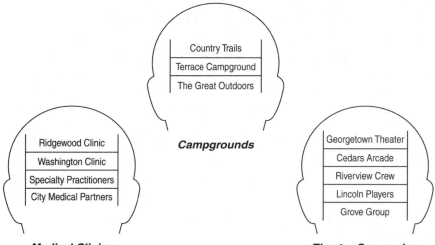

Constructed using design methodologies in Ries, Al, and Jack Trout. 2001. Positioning: The battle for your mind. 20th anniversary ed. New York: McGraw-Hill.

FIGURE 18-2 A Series of Product Ladders for Nonprofit Offerings

medical clinics, campgrounds, and theater companies. The products occupying the top rungs of these Product Ladders represent those offerings that the consumer views as most favorable in their respective product categories. Products at lower levels, however, are not as highly regarded by the consumer.

Of course, these particular Product Ladders represent the perceptions of only one individual whose views may or may not coincide with prevailing perceptions in the market. Nonprofit executives seeking more extensive, and thus useful, perspectives of consumer perceptions would need to acquire representative samples of product rankings for given product categories from targeted consumers. The data could then be aggregated and used to construct "market representative" Product Ladders that nonprofit executives could, in turn, use to determine strategic and tactical priorities.

MOVING UP THE PRODUCT LADDER

Nonprofit executives whose products occupy lower-level positions face an extremely difficult challenge as they pursue the top steps of Product Ladders. Although the outright dislodging of top-rung brands is usually impossible, nonprofit executives can make inroads toward these positions by relating their products to market-leading offerings.

A newly established kindergarten, for example, might feature in its advertisements its enhanced level of educational resources in relation to the market's leading kindergarten. A workforce development center might tout in its advertisements that it is able to place clients in positions of employment more quickly than the leading center in the market. A newly established healthy lifestyles web forum might feature in its marketing communications its advanced learning resources, superior panel of experts, and more elaborate user interface relative to the market leader's offering. By relating lower-rung products to market-leading offerings, nonprofit executives exploit consumer familiarity to leverage their own product positions.

NEW PRODUCTS AND THE PRODUCT LADDER

It should be mentioned that when nonprofit executives introduce *new-to-the-world products*, those products that define entirely new product categories never before offered to the public, consumers must formulate new

Product Ladders in their minds. Nonprofit executives can assist consumers in the construction of these new Product Ladders by relating totally new product offerings to existing products. Ries and Trout note that this approach was used with the introduction of the automobile, which was initially referred to as a horseless carriage, allowing consumers a familiar point of reference to understand and evaluate the new-to-the-world product offering. Once again, nonprofit executives exploit familiarity to gain a foothold in the minds of consumers.

SUMMARY

Ries and Trout's Product Ladder provides nonprofit executives with a useful tool for understanding the manner in which consumers perceive products in relation to competitive offerings. Notably, this tool directs attention to the fact that consumers rank products in their minds, with higher rankings indicating more favorable product offerings. The useful insights generated by the Product Ladder provide great assistance to nonprofit executives in their endeavors to achieve prominent positions for their product offerings in the minds of consumers.

EXERCISES

1. Define and comprehensively discuss Ries and Trout's Product Ladder, providing insights regarding its uses, features, meaning, and value, accompanied by an appropriate illustration. Be sure to include in your discussion an overview of the instrument's importance as a target marketing device in the nonprofit sector.
2. Select a particular nonprofit category (e.g., zoological parks, museums) and investigate all offerings available in a particular region. Then, based on your insights regarding the given establishments, construct a Product Ladder for the particular nonprofit category. Provide a brief narrative explaining your illustration.

REFERENCE

Ries, A., & Trout, J. (2001). *Positioning: The battle for your mind* (20th anniversary ed.). New York, NY: McGraw-Hill.

PART IV

Consumer Behavior and Product Promotions Tools

Abraham Maslow's Hierarchy of Needs

INTRODUCTION

Motivations to purchase and consume nonprofit offerings are as complex and varied as the number of goods and services available in the market-place. These motivations are fueled by an equally complex and varied array of human wants and needs, which nonprofit executives seek to address through the development and distribution of goods and services.

Different issues, events, and circumstances spark different motivations that require different interventions (i.e., goods and services). Given this, it is essential for nonprofit executives to possess a thorough understanding of human motivation.

One leading theory of human motivation was developed by Abraham Maslow, who theorized that all human needs can be grouped into one of five hierarchical categories—physiological, safety, social, esteem, and self-actualization—and that needs at one level will not motivate a person until needs at the preceding level have been satisfied. In other words, physiological needs must be satisfied before safety needs will become motivators, safety needs must be satisfied before social needs will become motivators, social needs must be satisfied before esteem needs will become motivators, and so on.

Illustrated in Figure 19-1, Maslow's Hierarchy of Needs is depicted as a pyramid consisting of five hierarchical levels representing different categories of human needs. These categories, accompanied by nonprofit-sector examples, are identified as follows.

PHYSIOLOGICAL NEEDS

Physiological needs represent basic human needs that are required for survival, including air, food, water, and health. Perhaps the best examples of nonprofit entities engaged in filling needs at this particular level are those

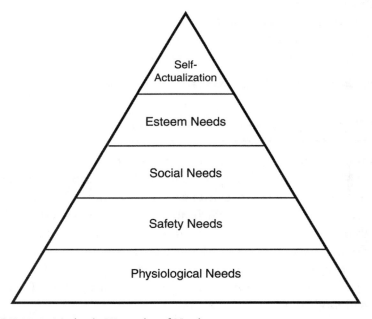

FIGURE 19-1 Maslow's Hierarchy of Needs

focused on the provision of food and water to the needy. Recipients of such assistance are quite varied, ranging from those suffering from long-term economic hardships to those temporarily inconvenienced by natural disasters. These organizations are indeed in the business of increasing the survival prospects of their clientele.

Life-saving interventions, such as ambulance transportation and emergency department services, also provide excellent examples of nonprofit offerings that satisfy physiological needs. The same could be said of labor and delivery services for expectant mothers and well-baby checkups for infants. Without such services, medical complications are more likely to occur, possibly resulting in injury or death. Each of these interventions is conducted for physiological purposes.

SAFETY NEEDS

Safety needs represent human needs for security and protection. Shelters providing accommodations for the homeless, battered women, runaways, and so on serve as excellent examples of nonprofit product offerings that address the safety and security needs of individuals.

Safety-oriented products that are applicable to broad society include offerings in the realm of domestic protection, such as police and fire services, which offer assistance, comfort, and peace of mind to the citizenry. Health insurance, much of which is provided by nonprofit entities, offers yet another example of a service that addresses the safety and security needs of individuals. These products offer individuals the peace of mind of knowing that they are protected.

SOCIAL NEEDS

Social needs involve human needs for love, friendship, affiliation, and acceptance by others. Civic clubs certainly are in the business of addressing the social needs of their members. The same could be said of churches, which provide numerous opportunities for individuals to interact with one another as they go about worshipping.

Perhaps less obvious would be those charitable organizations that provide guide dogs, wheelchairs, prosthetic devices, and other assistive products to those in need. These product offerings enable the injured and disabled to engage in society and interact more easily with others.

ESTEEM NEEDS

Esteem needs represent human needs for pride and prestige, as well as attention and recognition from others. Colleges and universities, for example, could be seen as fulfilling needs at this particular level. The attainment of undergraduate and graduate degrees, for example, yields many benefits for associated recipients; one being the prestige of carrying a noteworthy credential, which often increases one's self-confidence, pride, and general appeal. Membership levels provided by various associations, secured through extended tenure, skill mastery demonstrations, and so on, also serve as examples of offerings that address esteem needs. Such achievements bolster feelings of self-worth and much more.

SELF-ACTUALIZATION NEEDS

Self-actualization needs represent human needs for personal growth and fulfillment, and the nonprofit marketplace offers rich opportunities for individuals to satisfy these desires. Donations of time (through volunteerism) and money (through financial contributions) to local soup kitchens, homeless shelters, and other charitable organizations are examples of nonprofit sector opportunities that allow individuals to fulfill self-actualization needs. When individuals reach this level, they are operating at their pinnacle.

OPERATIONAL MATTERS

Maslow's Hierarchy of Needs is perhaps most useful to nonprofit executives as a tool for conceptualizing the underlying wants and needs—collectively termed *needs* by Maslow—that drive consumption of goods and services. By possessing a better understanding of the wants and needs satisfied by particular products, the underlying associated motivations, and the hierarchical order of the corresponding needs categories, nonprofit executives are better prepared to formulate promotional campaigns and engage in ongoing product management responsibilities.

Although Maslow theorized that higher-level needs will not motivate individuals until lower-level needs have been satisfied, he acknowledged that variations are possible and do occur. One could easily envision a situation where a person might decide to use his or her resources to pay for a membership in a social club (i.e., a social need, or perhaps an esteem need, depending on the particular membership and organization) rather than to secure an adequate health insurance policy (i.e., a safety need). This example illustrates that priorities among individuals often differ and may lead to unique pursuits.

SUMMARY

Maslow's Hierarchy of Needs serves as a simple, yet highly effective, tool for understanding human motivation. This tool is particularly useful in the nonprofit sector where motivations to consume the seemingly endless array of goods and services are driven by an equally intensive array of wants and needs.

Quite obviously, nonprofit executives can greatly improve marketing results if they understand how their product offerings fit into the overall scheme of human motivation. By understanding human motivation, nonprofit executives can better devise promotional campaigns that emphasize the attributes of associated product offerings in the context of the wants and needs that drive exchange, thus increasing the likelihood of marketing success.

EXERCISES

1. Provide a detailed overview of Maslow's Hierarchy of Needs, identifying and explaining its theoretical underpinnings, structure, features, and benefits. Support this overview by drawing an illustration of the hierarchy. Be sure to discuss the model's implications for nonprofit executives and their associated institutions.

2. Select a series of 10 nonprofit entities in your local market and identify what you would consider to be the key product offering associated with each. Then, prepare a diagram identifying the five categories listed in Maslow's Hierarchy of Needs and place the noted products in their appropriate categories. Provide an overview of your rationale for placing the products in the diagram as you did and provide details as to how you might go about marketing each of these offerings.

REFERENCES

Maslow, A. H. (1970). *Motivation and personality* (2nd ed.). New York, NY: Harper & Row.

Maslow, A. H. (1943). A theory of human motivation. *Psychological Review, 50,* 370–396.

CHAPTER 20

Everett Rogers' Diffusion of Innovations Model

LEARNING OBJECTIVES

After examining this chapter, readers will have the ability to:

- Understand that consumers vary in their willingness to adopt new product offerings, with some being quicker to adopt than others.
- Recognize that earlier adopters possess characteristics that are different from later adopters.
- Understand the benefits that earlier adopters provide to nonprofit executives as hasteners of the innovation diffusion process.
- Realize that personal issues, events, and circumstances often influence one's willingness to adopt new goods and services.
- Appreciate the value of Everett Rogers' Diffusion of Innovations Model as a tool for understanding the product adoption tendencies of consumers.

INTRODUCTION

Innovations—new goods and services that significantly enhance or improve one or more aspects of life—are usually not adopted by all members of a target market simultaneously. Instead, acceptance of these new products occurs gradually over time, through a process referred to as *diffusion*.

Emergent situations aside, consumers vary in their willingness to adopt new products. Some are quick to embrace new offerings, while others are less inclined to do so. Those who eagerly accept new products possess characteristics that are different from those who delay adoption. To understand the unique characteristics of adopters and their levels of innovativeness, nonprofit executives frequently turn to Everett Rogers' Diffusion of Innovations Model.

Illustrated in Figure 20-1, Rogers' Diffusion of Innovations Model is depicted as a bell-shaped curve that represents the adoption of an innovation over time. The model categorizes individuals as innovators, early adopters, early majority, late majority, or laggards based on when they adopt an innovation. These adopter categories are described as follows.

INNOVATORS

Described as "venturesome," innovators represent the first 2.5% of adopters. These individuals are comfortable with risk and uncertainty and are also typically wealthy—a prerequisite given that they must have the ability to absorb losses in the event that innovations fail to meet expectations. Although they are rarely community opinion leaders, innovators are instrumental in the diffusion process because of their willingness to quickly adopt new goods and services. Their initial usage experiences indirectly promote innovations to other consumers in the market, building product awareness and ultimately hastening the diffusion process.

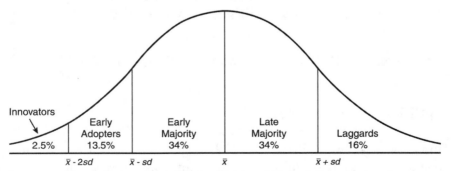

FIGURE 20-1 Rogers' Diffusion of Innovations Model

EARLY ADOPTERS

Early adopters are characterized by "respect," and they make up the next 13.5% of adopters. They are community opinion leaders who command the respect of their peers, who look to these early adopters for advice on whether they, too, should adopt innovations. Early adopters serve as information disseminators in that, upon adoption of product offerings, they are quick to convey their experiences to others. Given these characteristics, it is quite obvious that early adopters play an essential role in the diffusion process.

EARLY MAJORITY

Members of the early majority are described as "deliberate," and they represent the next 34% of adopters. These individuals are rarely opinion leaders, but they do actively interact with their peers. They tend to deliberate for some time before they adopt new products. Early majority members do not want to be the first or the last to adopt innovations.

LATE MAJORITY

Members of the late majority are described as "skeptical," and they make up the next 34% of adopters. These cautious individuals are leery of new ideas and often only adopt innovations under peer pressure. Their reluctance to adopt innovations is related to their relatively scarce resources, necessitating that late majority members delay adoption until new product uncertainties are removed.

LAGGARDS

Laggards are described as "traditional," and they represent the last 16% of adopters. These individuals are suspicious of new products and are highly resistant to change of any kind. They are almost never opinion leaders and have very limited marketplace interactions. Like members of the late majority, laggards possess few resources—a factor that reduces their willingness to adopt innovations until new product uncertainties are eliminated.

OPERATIONAL MATTERS

Research suggests that differences between earlier and later adopters are quite pronounced, as illustrated in Table 20-1. By targeting earlier adopters of innovations, significant new-product publicity can be generated through their extensive informal networks. This increased publicity hastens the innovation diffusion process at no cost to organizations, making earlier adopters very desirable targets for cost-conscious nonprofit executives seeking to maximize their promotions resources.

Of course, there are situations in the marketplace where instant, market-wide innovation adoption would be expected. Many innovations are consumed not out of desire but out of need, which tends to hasten the diffusion process. Individuals who have been involved in automobile accidents, for example, would hardly discourage a fire department's use of innovative devices to aid in occupant extraction, nor would they discourage the receipt of innovative emergency medical services. Likewise, unemployed individuals who are unfamiliar with web technologies and do not care to incorporate them into their daily lives would likely immediately immerse themselves in such technologies if their local job placement center required that employment applications be completed exclusively online.

Table 20-1 Differences between Earlier and Later Adopters

Earlier adopters have more years of formal education than later adopters.

Earlier adopters have higher social status than later adopters.

Earlier adopters have a greater degree of upward social mobility than later adopters.

Earlier adopters have greater intelligence than later adopters.

Earlier adopters have a more favorable attitude toward change than later adopters.

Earlier adopters are better able to cope with uncertainty and risk than later adopters.

Earlier adopters have a more favorable attitude toward science than later adopters.

Earlier adopters are more highly interconnected through interpersonal networks in their social system than later adopters.

Earlier adopters are more cosmopolite than later adopters.

Earlier adopters have greater exposure to mass media communications channels than later adopters.

Earlier adopters seek information about innovations more actively than later adopters.

Earlier adopters have a higher degree of opinion leadership than later adopters.

Source: Derived from information in Rogers, E. M. (1995). *Diffusion of innovations* (4th ed.). New York, NY: The Free Press.

Innovation adoption can also be hastened by governmental regulations that encourage or mandate the adoption of new offerings for the benefit of special populations (e.g., school cafeteria meals that meet certain dietary guidelines) or broad society (e.g., the use of energy-saving light bulbs placed in virtually any facility, including those operated by nonprofit entities). Clearly, such circumstances and events act as innovation adoption catalysts.

SUMMARY

The innovation-rich marketplace necessitates that nonprofit executives possess a thorough understanding of the innovation diffusion process. Rogers' Diffusion of Innovations Model yields significant insights into the unique characteristics of adopters and their levels of innovativeness. This tool allows nonprofit executives to better understand their customers and more effectively design promotional campaigns that expedite the innovation diffusion process.

EXERCISES

1. Prepare a detailed overview of Everett Rogers' Diffusion of Innovations Model, describing each of the five identified consumer groups and their innovation adoption tendencies. Share your thoughts regarding the tool's implications and uses in the nonprofit sector.
2. Place yourself in the top leadership role of a newly established nonprofit entity offering a product of your choice. Based on your knowledge of Everett Rogers' Diffusion of Innovations Model, develop a strategy for acquiring patronage. What group or groups would you target and why? How would you go about reaching these designated groups? What additional steps would you take to ensure maximum patronage?

REFERENCE

Rogers, E. M. (1995). *Diffusion of innovations* (4th ed.). New York, NY: The Free Press.

CHAPTER 21

The DAGMAR Marketing Communications Spectrum

LEARNING OBJECTIVES

After examining this chapter, readers will have the ability to:

- Understand that marketing success depends extensively on successfully communicating with current and potential customers.
- Appreciate the intricacies of the communications process.
- Realize the options available for communicating with target markets, as identified in the marketing promotions mix.
- Recognize that when consumers adopt new products, the act of adoption is rarely a singular event.
- Understand the successive stages of the adoption process, ultimately leading to action, as identified in the DAGMAR Marketing Communications Spectrum.

INTRODUCTION

Society has become reliant on the seemingly endless array of innovations that routinely enter the marketplace. Such innovations have not only become commonplace, but they also have become expected and even demanded by the public. The extensive range of innovative goods and services can be overwhelming, with new offerings constantly entering the marketplace.

It might seem as though success would be guaranteed simply by developing and providing new and improved goods and services. However, an equally important prerequisite for success involves the effective communication of new offerings to potential customers. If customers are not aware of new and improved products, one could hardly expect the offerings to achieve success.

New and improved goods and services can and do fail, often as a result of failed communications efforts. Clearly, nonprofit executives must endeavor to use good communicative techniques in their attempts to build consumer awareness of their product offerings.

THE MECHANICS OF COMMUNICATION

The awareness-building process is a process of communication, an aspect of product management that falls under the promotions component of the marketing mix. Successes in promotion are the direct result of successes in communication. As illustrated in Figure 21-1, the communications process involves two parties: a sender and a receiver. The sender's objective is to deliver his or her intended message to the receiver. To do this, the sender encodes the message, which is sent via selected media—the communications channel or channels through which the message is delivered—to the receiver. The receiver then decodes the message and, if inclined to do so,

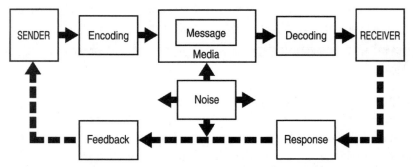

From Kotler, Philip. Marketing Management, 11th Edition, © 2003. Adapted by permission of Pearson Education, Inc., Upper Saddle River, NJ. Reprinted by permission.

FIGURE 21-1 The Communications Process

encodes a response that is returned to the sender as feedback. Feedback from the receiver may take many forms, including requests for additional information, acceptances or rejections of sales proposals, and purchases of goods and services.

Throughout the communications process, message distortion and/or elimination may occur due to negative environmental influences, collectively referred to as *noise* (e.g., competitive messages, distractions). Although the communications process seems quite simple, in reality it is among the most complex of processes and must be mastered for marketing success. Clearly, the ability of nonprofit executives to successfully communicate with current and potential customers greatly improves the marketplace experiences of associated product offerings.

THE DAGMAR MARKETING COMMUNICATIONS SPECTRUM

Emergent situations aside, when consumers adopt new products, the act of adoption is rarely a singular event. Singularity of the process would not be expected, of course, because consumers must gain familiarity with new product offerings, determining, among other things, the potential benefits that might be offered by the associated goods and services. Instead, adoption consists of a series of progressive steps leading up to the purchase and consumption of new products.

To understand the adoption process, nonprofit executives frequently turn to the DAGMAR Marketing Communications Spectrum. DAGMAR is an acronym for *Defining Advertising Goals for Measured Advertising Results*, the title of the book that presents the spectrum. Illustrated in Figure 21-2, the DAGMAR Marketing Communications Spectrum divides the adoption process into five sequential levels or stages: unawareness, awareness, comprehension, conviction, and action. Each of these stages is influenced by marketing forces and countervailing forces, which are depicted by arrows in the diagram. The stages of the DAGMAR Marketing Communications Spectrum are explained as follows.

Stage 1: Unawareness
During the unawareness stage, consumers are oblivious to the existence of new goods and services. Any promotional messages that have been disseminated have not successfully reached consumers.

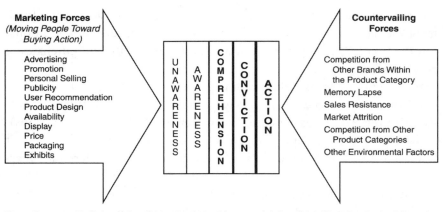

From Dagmar: Defining Advertising Goals for Measured Advertising Results, 2nd ed. by Solomon Dutka. (1st ed. by Russell Colley). Copyright © 1995 by NTC Publishing Group. Published by NTC Business Books.

FIGURE 21-2   The DAGMAR Marketing Communications Spectrum

Stage 2: Awareness

Consumers first become aware of the existence of new products during the awareness stage. Here, they also gain a general understanding of the potential benefits associated with new offerings. At this point, consumers possess a base level of knowledge regarding new products but little more. They cannot recall, for example, the entities that produce and provide the offerings, associated locations of availability, and so on.

Stage 3: Comprehension

During the comprehension stage, consumers gain a detailed understanding of new products. Consumers are able to recall, for example, the entities that produce and provide the offerings, associated features and benefits, locations of availability, packaging, brand names, and logos.

Stage 4: Conviction

During the conviction stage, consumers develop strong beliefs regarding the virtues of new products. Here, preferences for new offerings are formulated. Consumers have filtered through the information gained from prior stages of the spectrum and have become reasonably confident that the associated products will meet or exceed their expectations.

Stage 5: Action
The DAGMAR Marketing Communications Spectrum concludes with the action stage where consumers decide to adopt (i.e., purchase and consume) new product offerings.

ENCOURAGING ACTION

Beyond identification of the stages of adoption, the DAGMAR Marketing Communications Spectrum illustrates the influences that marketing forces and countervailing forces have on consumers throughout the adoption process. Marketing forces (e.g., product design, pricing, advertising, personal selling, publicity) seek to move consumers toward action, while countervailing forces (e.g., competition, memory lapse, sales resistance, market attrition) seek to drive consumers away from action. Nonprofit executives must strive to develop promotional campaigns that will effectively neutralize countervailing forces and move consumers toward action in as expeditious a fashion as possible.

The exact composition of any promotional campaign is, of course, dependent on the specific nature of the products being marketed. In their quest to entice target markets to purchase and consume products, nonprofit executives normally promote goods and services using a variety of methods.

The array of methods used by nonprofit executives to communicate product information to customers is referred to as the *promotions mix*. Also termed the *communications mix*, this array is identified in Figure 21-3 and defined in Table 21-1. Advertising tends to be used universally by all types of nonprofit entities (e.g., schools and colleges, museums, trade associations, medical clinics). However, some entities are more reliant on particular forms of promotion (e.g., direct marketing by those entities engaged in soliciting charitable contributions). Each promotional method possesses strengths and weaknesses and must be studied carefully to ensure compatibility with the products to be marketed.

When promotional methods have been selected, nonprofit executives must make additional decisions, many of which are specific to particular promotions vehicles. Advertising, for example, involves a variety of unique points of consideration that Philip Kotler termed the *five Ms of advertising*, illustrated in Figure 21-4. Regardless of the communicative tools utilized, the goal of any promotional campaign is to move

Table 21-1 Promotions Mix: Definitions and Examples

Advertising	A promotional method involving the paid use of mass media to deliver messages.
	Examples include newspaper, magazine, radio, television, and billboard advertisements.
Personal Selling	A promotional method involving the use of a sales force to convey messages.
	Examples include sales representatives and account executives.
Sales Promotion	A promotional method involving the use of incentives to stimulate consumer interest.
	Examples include discount coupons, free gifts, samples, and contests.
Public Relations	A promotional method involving the use of publicity and other unpaid forms of promotion to deliver messages.
	Examples include press releases, open houses, facility tours, and educational seminars.
Direct Marketing	A promotional method involving the delivery of messages directly to consumers.
	Examples include direct-mail marketing, telemarketing, and catalog marketing.

FIGURE 21-3 The Promotions Mix

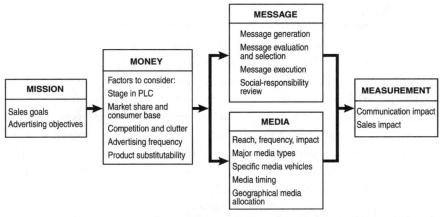

From Kotler, Philip. Marketing Management, 11th Edition, © 2003. Adapted by permission of Pearson Education, Inc., Upper Saddle River, NJ. Reprinted by permission.

FIGURE 21-4 Kotler's Five Ms of Advertising

consumers through the successive stages of the DAGMAR Marketing Communications Spectrum as swiftly as possible.

CONTINUED PRODUCT USE

It should be noted that although the DAGMAR Marketing Communications Spectrum concludes with product adoption, nonprofit executives must not neglect customers after the adoption decision. Continued use of product offerings by customers is as important as the initial adoption of the associated goods and services. Nonprofit executives must, therefore, strive to ensure that post-adoption attention is not neglected.

A medical center's maternity services department that neglects the wants and needs of an expectant mother will almost certainly lose the trust and the future business of this new mother and possibly that of her network of friends. A museum that neglects the programmatic and exhibition preferences of its patrons will almost certainly lose the trust and the future business of these individuals and possibly that of their network of friends, courtesy of negative word-of-mouth communications. Clearly, post-adoption support is imperative for enduring marketing success.

SUMMARY

The DAGMAR Marketing Communications Spectrum clearly illustrates the successive steps that consumers pass through toward the purchase and consumption of new goods and services, giving attention to the influences forwarded by marketing forces and countervailing forces. Among other things, the spectrum serves as a useful reminder of the necessity to effectively communicate with target markets. Such effective communication neutralizes countervailing forces and moves consumers toward action. The more expeditiously consumers move through the stages of the DAGMAR Marketing Communications Spectrum, the quicker the occurrence of exchange and resulting marketing success.

EXERCISES

1. Define and comprehensively discuss the DAGMAR Marketing Communications Spectrum, its successive stages leading to action, and the marketing forces and countervailing forces that influence movement through these stages. A diagram of the spectrum should be included to add value to your narrative. Be sure to include in your discussion details regarding the importance of communicating effectively with target audiences in the nonprofit sector.
2. Place yourself in the top leadership role of a newly established nonprofit entity offering a product of your choice. Develop a communications strategy for addressing target audiences during each of the stages of the DAGMAR Marketing Communications Spectrum, indicating how you plan to hasten the purchase and consumption of your given product offering. Also reflect on what actions you might take to ensure post-adoption attention and support.

REFERENCES

Dutka, S. (1995). *DAGMAR: Defining advertising goals for measured advertising results* (2nd ed.). Lincolnwood, IL: NTC Business Books.

Kotler, P. (2003). *Marketing management* (11th ed.). Upper Saddle River, NJ: Prentice Hall.

CHAPTER 22

Raphel & Raphel's Loyalty Ladder

LEARNING OBJECTIVES

After examining this chapter, readers will have the ability to:

- Understand that the patronage of customers is vital to institutional survival, growth, and prosperity.
- Realize that long-term relationships with customers yield lasting benefits for nonprofit entities.
- Recognize that the pursuit of customer loyalty represents a worthwhile marketing goal.
- Appreciate Raphel and Raphel's Loyalty Ladder as a tool for understanding the loyalty-building process.

INTRODUCTION

Nonprofit entities are ultimately dependent on customers and their continued patronage for survival, growth, and prosperity. This dependency applies even in those situations where the actual service recipients are not the paying parties; someone is covering the associated costs and, in doing so, requires that clientele groups are addressed appropriately.

Nonprofit executives must focus significant attention on addressing the wants and needs of target markets through the provision of effective product solutions. When nonprofit executives select target markets, they must diligently pursue these groups in an effort to gain their patronage.

Beyond individual transactions, however, they ideally seek to establish long-term relationships with their target audiences.

If nonprofit executives can gain a loyal following of customers, long-term success becomes a distinct possibility. Hence, they must possess a thorough understanding of loyalty and the methods for its attainment. To gain insight into the loyalty-building process, nonprofit executives frequently refer to Raphel and Raphel's Loyalty Ladder.

Illustrated in Figure 22-1, Raphel and Raphel's Loyalty Ladder is depicted as a series of five steps—prospects, shoppers, customers, clients, and advocates—representing progressive levels of customer loyalty. The steps of the Loyalty Ladder are explained as follows.

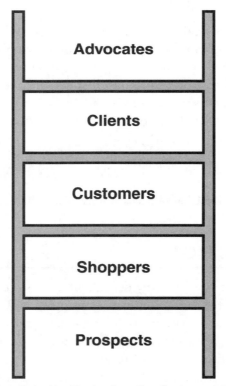

Adapted from Up the Loyalty Ladder: Turning Sometime Customers into Full-Time Advocates of Your Business by Murray Raphel and Neil Raphel. Copyright © 1995 by Neil Raphel and Murray Raphel. Published by HarperBusiness. Reprinted by permission of Neil Raphel.

FIGURE 22-1   Raphel & Raphel's Loyalty Ladder

PROSPECTS

Individuals who potentially have wants and needs for the goods and services of particular nonprofit entities are considered prospects. At this step, individuals may or may not be aware of given nonprofit entities and products. Regardless, purchase and/or patronage activity has not occurred.

A new private academy providing K–12 education is immersed within an environment of prospects. The same could be said of a local zoological park that recently opened for business. Other examples would include a sheltered workshop that produces home furnishings and a nonprofit foundation that bakes and sells gourmet cookies for the purpose of generating resources for a worthy cause. Each of these entities must entice prospects to forward their patronage for associated current and future needs. To do this, nonprofit executives must convey the attributes of their various product offerings to consumers through the use of marketing communications (e.g., advertising, sales promotion, public relations).

SHOPPERS

Individuals who advance beyond the prospect stage and inquire about the goods and services offered by entities are considered shoppers. Shoppers have learned of organizations and associated product offerings and are debating about extending their patronage.

People shop for both goods and services. The tangible nature of goods allows consumers to see and touch these offerings. Individuals, for example, can visit the retail outlets of sheltered workshops to see, touch, and handle produced furnishings directly. They can see, touch, and taste the gourmet cookies sold by charitable organizations as a means of revenue generation.

Individuals also shop for services, albeit in a different manner. Perhaps they noticed a television advertisement announcing the grand opening celebration of a new private academy and decided to attend the event to learn more. Perhaps they received a direct-mail piece promoting the new zoological park in the community and it sparked their interest. If shoppers believe that the products under consideration will meet or exceed their expectations, they will advance to the next rung of the Loyalty Ladder—they become customers.

CUSTOMERS

When individuals purchase and consume the goods and services offered by organizations, they become customers. Perhaps an individual decides to purchase a coffee table from a sheltered workshop. Perhaps a family decides to buy several boxes of gourmet cookies from a given charitable organization. With these transactions, both establishments have gained customers.

As for services, perhaps the parents of a third-grader decide to enroll their child in the new private academy after learning more at the institution's grand opening celebration. With this enrollment, the academy has gained a new customer. If the recipient of the local zoological park's direct-mail piece decides to visit, the zoo has gained a new customer. If these entities successfully meet and exceed the customer's expectations, the individual may become a repeat customer and graduate to the next rung of the Loyalty Ladder—the client.

CLIENTS

Clients are those individuals who *regularly* purchase goods and services from given organizations. A person who made a prior purchase of a home furnishing from a sheltered workshop and returns to make subsequent purchases would be considered a client. A family who regularly purchases cookies during a nonprofit foundation's annual cookie sales fundraising drive also would be considered a client.

Similarly on the service side, a parent who continues to enroll his or her child in a particular academy as he or she advances through the available grades would be considered a client. The same would be said of an individual who routinely visits his or her local zoological park for the entertainment and enjoyment of the experience.

Importantly, entities must not take the patronage of clients for granted. Organizations must ensure that they continue to offer the same quality and service that originally converted customers into clients. Clients are extremely valuable to the entities they frequent. They become even more valuable if they can be converted into advocates.

ADVOCATES

Advocates are individuals who have been so impressed with given establishments and associated product offerings that they openly encourage others to extend their patronage. If a client of a sheltered workshop that produces home furnishings openly communicates the virtues of the given establishment to coworkers, family members, and friends, the client becomes an advocate of the sheltered workshop. If a client actively seeks to encourage his or her friends to buy cookies from a given nonprofit foundation, that person becomes an advocate of the foundation.

Client parents who entice neighbors to send their children to a given private academy become advocates of that academy. The same advocate status would be bestowed upon the client of a zoological park who begins referring family and friends to the zoo.

Advocates stand at the top of the Loyalty Ladder. They are the most valuable patrons of establishments for an obvious reason: through their testimonials to others, advocates generate new patrons for nonprofit entities.

OPERATIONAL MATTERS

According to Raphel and Raphel, individuals are always prospects, frequently shoppers, often customers, sometimes clients, and rarely advocates. This statement succinctly illustrates that the more beneficial patrons, those occupying the top steps of the Loyalty Ladder, are not as common as their less valuable counterparts.

Fortunately, nonprofit executives can take steps to advance their customer base to higher levels of the Loyalty Ladder. This progression can be achieved by (1) producing and providing goods and services that meet and exceed the expectations of patrons, and (2) embracing a customer service orientation that is championed by all employees.

Typical examples of activities that are likely to convert prospects ultimately into advocates include operating clean and well-organized establishments, providing the latest product innovations, addressing customer inquiries in a timely manner, and ensuring that staff members are helpful and courteous.

By engaging in these activities, nonprofit entities are communicating to visitors that they are committed to excellence. Nonprofit entities that invest in institutional excellence will undoubtedly be rewarded by the resulting loyalty of valuable patrons occupying the upper levels of the Loyalty Ladder.

SUMMARY

Raphel and Raphel's Loyalty Ladder provides nonprofit executives with a useful method for visualizing the progressive levels of customer loyalty. This tool serves as a reminder of the need for nonprofit entities to produce and provide top-quality goods and services, along with ever-increasing levels of customer service, in an effort to boost individuals to progressively higher and more prosperous rungs of the Loyalty Ladder.

EXERCISES

1. Define and comprehensively discuss Raphel and Raphel's Loyalty Ladder, identifying and explaining its theoretical underpinnings, structure, features, and benefits. Support this overview by drawing an illustration of the Loyalty Ladder. Share your thoughts regarding the tool's implications and uses in the nonprofit sector.
2. Select a nonprofit product of your choice for placement in your local market and envision its key features and benefits. Then, prepare a detailed list of innovative techniques for advancing consumers up the steps of Raphel and Raphel's Loyalty Ladder. How do you intend to keep patrons in and around the highest rung of the Loyalty Ladder?

REFERENCE

Raphel, M., & Raphel, N. (1995). *Up the loyalty ladder: Turning sometime customers into full-time advocates of your business*. New York, NY: HarperBusiness.

CHAPTER 23

Bernd Schmitt's CEM Framework

LEARNING OBJECTIVES

After examining this chapter, readers will have the ability to:

- Understand the historical progression of marketing, from a discipline initially focused on production, to one concentrating on sales, and finally, in present times, to one focused on customer wants and needs.
- Recognize the importance of focusing on the wants and needs of customers, permitting such to guide marketing decisions.
- Realize that mutual benefits are afforded to nonprofit entities and their respective customer populations by designing and managing all-encompassing customer experiences.
- Appreciate the innovative guidance for the assembly and management of customer experiences provided by Bernd Schmitt's CEM (Customer Experience Management) Framework.

INTRODUCTION

Proficiently addressing the wants and needs of customers stands as one of the greatest challenges facing nonprofit executives. Those who consistently meet and exceed customer expectations are rewarded with lasting patronage and the accompanying results of growth and prosperity. Those who fail in this regard, however, find themselves with a dwindling customer base and the accompanying results of institutional decline and, ultimately, failure.

The discipline of marketing has made great strides over time to place the customer first in all aspects of operation. Early efforts tended to focus on issues such as production (i.e., the production concept) and sales (i.e., the sales concept), viewing customer expectations as secondary matters. As the discipline progressed, however, entities began to understand and appreciate the role of customers in marketing, realizing that focusing attention on meeting and exceeding the wants and needs of target audiences would yield significant mutual benefits—a philosophy referred to as the marketing concept.

Today, marketing efforts are clearly focused on customers, with robust initiatives in the areas of customer satisfaction (i.e., the marketing practice of meeting and, ideally, exceeding the wants and needs of customers), customer relationship management (i.e., the marketing practice of delivering personalized attention, service, and support to target audiences in an effort to establish lasting bonds with customers, ensuring their enduring patronage), and so on.

Such efforts have unquestionably improved the marketing performance of establishments, but future gains will require continued innovations. One particular innovation is offered by Bernd Schmitt, who advocates embracing an approach that completely envelopes target audiences through the design and management of comprehensive customer experiences. This innovation, presented in Table 23-1, is known as the CEM (Customer Experience Management) Framework.

Schmitt's CEM Framework consists of a series of five steps—analyzing the experiential world of the customer (an analysis step), building the

---

Table 23-1 Schmitt's CEM Framework

Step 1: Analyzing the experiential world of the customer

Step 2: Building the experiential platform

Step 3: Designing the brand experience

Step 4: Structuring the customer interface

Step 5: Engaging in continuous innovation

Source: Derived from information in Schmitt, B. H. (2003). *Customer experience management: A revolutionary approach to connecting with your customers*. Hoboken, NJ: Wiley.

experiential platform (a strategy step), designing the brand experience (an implementation step), structuring the customer interface (an implementation step), and engaging in continuous innovation (an implementation step)—which ultimately yields a complete and highly fulfilling customer experience.

As its name suggests, the CEM Framework focuses on *experience* rather than the traditional pursuit of *satisfaction*. A customer experience is multifaceted and, if well designed and managed, yields customer satisfaction, among other benefits. Hence, the development of productive and enjoyable customer experiences affords benefits to customers that eclipse those garnered via the traditional, but more limited, pursuit of customer satisfaction. The steps of Schmitt's CEM Framework are explained as follows.

STEP 1: ANALYZING THE EXPERIENTIAL WORLD OF THE CUSTOMER

The first step of Schmitt's CEM Framework involves the investigation and analysis of the experiential world of the customer. During this step, nonprofit executives are essentially seeking to develop an intensive knowledge of their customer base with the intention of understanding the types of experiences that their target audiences are seeking through the purchase and consumption of given goods and services.

To achieve an accurate understanding of customers and the experiences they desire, nonprofit executives must ensure that they have accurately defined their target audiences. They must then study the meaning of their product offerings and desired characteristics of delivery from the perspective of these groups. How, for example, do customers view given nonprofit entities and their products? What information requirements do customers have regarding given nonprofit goods and services? What can be done to ensure that customers receiving given nonprofit offerings have the most pleasing customer experience possible?

Coupling the information gained from customer-oriented inquiries with information regarding competitors and their customer experience initiatives yields significant insights. Such discoveries far eclipse those gained via traditional customer satisfaction assessment approaches, such as the customer satisfaction survey. Although traditional approaches remain valuable, enhanced details that yield comprehensive profiles of customers, their wants and needs, and their experiential preferences undoubtedly improve marketing outcomes.

STEP 2: BUILDING THE EXPERIENTIAL PLATFORM

The second step of Schmitt's CEM Framework involves the construction of experiential platforms for given product offerings based on discoveries identified in the previous step of the CEM Framework. Here, nonprofit executives take the information gained from customer analyses and formulate product delivery methods, known as *experiential platforms*, that are consistent with the experiences desired by their target audiences.

Importantly, experiential platforms must be thoroughly documented, as such platforms become the blueprints for delivering customer experiences. These platforms essentially stipulate the strategy that will be implemented through the remaining steps of the CEM Framework.

STEP 3: DESIGNING THE BRAND EXPERIENCE

Designing the brand experience represents the third step of Schmitt's CEM Framework. Here, nonprofit executives seek to convey the essence of their experiential platforms through the development of meaningful identity-related elements (e.g., logos, signage, packaging, advertisements) associated with given product offerings. Importantly, each element portraying these offerings must be formulated to convey, as richly as possible, defined experiential platforms. Conveyance of the experiences that customers can expect to receive as patrons is essential for marketing success under the CEM Framework, and branding initiatives offer immense opportunities to communicate such experiences.

STEP 4: STRUCTURING THE CUSTOMER INTERFACE

The fourth step of Schmitt's CEM Framework involves the design, development, and implementation of the infrastructure (i.e., the customer interface) that is instituted to ensure the exchange of information between organizations and their target audiences. Depending on the particular nonprofit product under examination, the nature of the exchange of information can be face-to-face (e.g., a marriage counselor speaking with a troubled couple, a minister preaching to a congregation, a professor lecturing to students in a classroom) or at a distance (e.g., an expert discussing nutrition on a healthy lifestyles web forum, a trade association providing continuing education courses via the Internet, a social worker counseling callers who contact a domestic violence hotline).

The customer interface is arguably the most important element associated with the delivery of experiential platforms. As with designing brands, structuring customer interfaces requires nonprofit executives to ensure that selected information-exchange vehicles support the experiential platforms that were defined earlier in the CEM Framework.

STEP 5: ENGAGING IN CONTINUOUS INNOVATION

The final step of Schmitt's CEM Framework involves the continual pursuit of innovation, with nonprofit executives striving to incorporate such advancements in a manner that will enhance not only their given product offerings but also the experiences afforded to customers, courtesy of the new discoveries.

New innovations in the nonprofit sector can be quite varied. Some may directly pertain to given nonprofit product offerings (e.g., new electronic database resources in a university library, enhanced transportation technologies provided by an ambulance company). Others may indirectly relate to nonprofit goods and services (e.g., breakthrough leadership innovations, improved institutional heating and air conditioning systems). Regardless of the particular innovations at hand, nonprofit executives must ensure that they stay abreast of the latest advancements in an effort to deliver both product and experiential value to customers.

OPERATIONAL MATTERS

When nonprofit executives implement the CEM Framework, they must remind themselves that their primary task is to study, design, and continually improve customer experiences within their establishments. Crafting the customer experience is the element that differentiates the CEM Framework from other customer-focused marketing initiatives.

By focusing on delivering a customer experience rather than a static event of customer satisfaction, opportunities to meet and exceed the expectations of customers are greatly enhanced. Clearly, nonprofit entities that incorporate the CEM Framework are well positioned to deliver enhanced value to customers, resulting in enduring patronage and its associated benefits.

SUMMARY

Schmitt's CEM Framework provides nonprofit executives with an innovative formula for advancing beyond static customer satisfaction initiatives and into the dynamic realm of delivering comprehensive customer experiences that completely immerse target audiences. Clearly, the CEM Framework can assist nonprofit executives in their endeavors to proficiently address the wants and needs of their target audiences.

EXERCISES

1. Provide a detailed overview of Bernd Schmitt's CEM Framework, noting facets regarding its purpose, use, and value in nonprofit organizations. Share your thoughts and ideas regarding the degree to which modern nonprofit entities arrange excellent customer experiences.
2. Place yourself in the top leadership role of a soon-to-be-launched nonprofit establishment of your choice in your local market. Briefly define the entity's mission and product array. Prepare a detailed plan of how you might go about delivering comprehensive customer experiences that immerse your target audiences. Be sure to indicate how your plan represents an improvement over standard customer service practices in today's nonprofit organizations.

REFERENCE

Schmitt, B. H. (2003). *Customer experience management: A revolutionary approach to connecting with your customers.* Hoboken, NJ: Wiley.

CHAPTER 24

Osgood, Suci, and Tannenbaum's Semantic Differential

INTRODUCTION

Despite the multitude of activities that nonprofit executives perform, they are ultimately charged with satisfying the wants and needs of their target markets through the provision of effective product solutions. Given this, nonprofit executives must thoroughly understand customers and their perceptions regarding product offerings.

A useful tool for assessing customer perceptions related to nonprofit offerings is known as the Semantic Differential, an objective method for measurement developed by Charles Osgood, George Suci, and Percy Tannenbaum. The Semantic Differential is a broad-based measurement tool that can be implemented in a wide variety of fashions depending on the associated research inquiries at hand. The broad-based nature of the Semantic Differential gives the tool enormous flexibility but requires that it be adapted to the specific given situations.

The Semantic Differential is best explained by viewing an example, such as that of a medical center seeking insights into customer perceptions, as shown in Figure 24-1. As depicted in Figure 24-1, the Semantic

What do you think?   **Jackson Medical Clinic**

For each of the following scales, place an "X" in the blank that best reflects your views regarding the given attribute. When completed, please return the survey to our front desk receptionist.

Convenient parking ___:___:___:___:___:___:___ Inconvenient parking

Convenient hours ___:___:___:___:___:___:___ Inconvenient hours

Convenient admitting ___:___:___:___:___:___:___ Inconvenient admitting

Short waiting times ___:___:___:___:___:___:___ Long waiting times

Clean facilities ___:___:___:___:___:___:___ Dirty facilities

Modern technology ___:___:___:___:___:___:___ Dated technology

Friendly staff members ___:___:___:___:___:___:___ Unfriendly staff members

Excellent patient care ___:___:___:___:___:___:___ Poor patient care

Excellent customer service ___:___:___:___:___:___:___ Poor customer service

Thank you for your participation!

Constructed using design methodologies in Osgood, Charles E., George J. Suci, and Percy H. Tannenbaum. 1957. The measurement of meaning. Urbana, IL: University of Illinois Press.

FIGURE 24-1 A Medical Clinic's Semantic Differential Survey

Differential is essentially a survey that presents a series of descriptive scales pertaining to perceptions associated with a particular good or service. The survey is distributed to customers or other applicable parties who are asked to judge the particular product based on the associated scales. Completed surveys are then averaged to reveal a single line, such as the one illustrated in Figure 24-2, which depicts the product perspectives of those who completed the survey.

The results of the medical clinic's survey, as depicted in Figure 24-2, clearly illustrate that the clinic is viewed very positively by its customer base in all areas except in regard to admitting and waiting time. With this

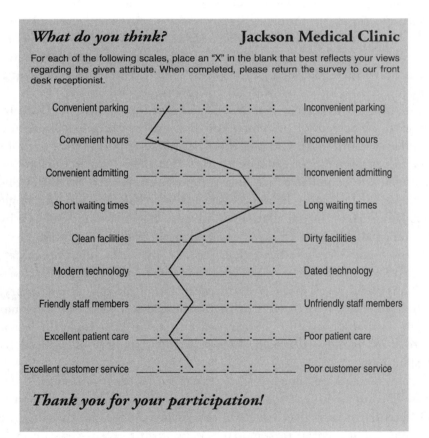

Constructed using design methodologies in Osgood, Charles E., George J. Suci, and Percy H. Tannenbaum. 1957. The measurement of meaning. Urbana, IL: University of Illinois Press.

FIGURE 24-2 A Medical Clinic's Semantic Differential Survey Results

information, the clinic can work to improve its performance in these areas. Admissions convenience might be increased by introducing an enhanced patient-information system. Waiting room delays might be reduced by increasing the clinic's staff of medical practitioners or by scheduling appointments more appropriately.

OPERATIONAL MATTERS

Clearly, the Semantic Differential offers nonprofit executives a convenient method for assessing customer perceptions related to given offerings. As illustrated in the previous example, this tool requires that nonprofit executives simply (1) formulate a series of scales related to a given offering, (2) prepare a survey depicting these scales, (3) distribute the survey to customers, and (4) average and illustrate survey results. The results of the Semantic Differential survey are then analyzed to determine the strengths and weaknesses associated with the product under evaluation.

In addition to its use as an assessment tool for the products held by entities, the Semantic Differential can also provide valuable insights into competitive offerings. Gaining this knowledge requires that nonprofit executives circulate an expanded survey that includes a section for respondents to complete concerning competitive products. If used in this manner, the results can be respectively averaged and displayed on a single diagram, such as the one illustrated in Figure 24-3 that was developed by a municipal golf course to assess competing offerings in the community.

The results clearly indicate that Capital City Golf Club, the evaluating entity, is perceived by survey respondents to be superior to Jackson Country Club in all areas, with the exception of the pro shop category, where its shop is perceived to be less desirable. With this information, Capital City Golf Club can concentrate on addressing the "poor pro shop" issue while maintaining the positive attributes noted by respondents.

Additionally, the Semantic Differential can be used to monitor progress. This monitoring is accomplished by circulating identical Semantic Differential surveys over time and comparing the results. By using the Semantic Differential in this manner, nonprofit executives gain even greater insights into operations.

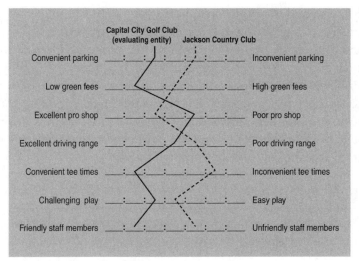

Constructed using design methodologies in Osgood, Charles E., George J. Suci, and Percy H. Tannenbaum. 1957. The measurement of meaning. Urbana, IL: University of Illinois Press.

FIGURE 24-3 Survey Results for Competing Golf Courses

SUMMARY

The Semantic Differential provides nonprofit executives with a highly flexible tool for understanding how customers perceive product offerings. With this information, they can take steps to build upon product strengths and reduce or eliminate associated weaknesses. By gaining a better understanding of consumer perceptions regarding products, nonprofit executives are better equipped to offer goods and services that satisfy the wants and needs of target markets.

EXERCISES

1. Provide a detailed overview of Osgood, Suci, and Tannenbaum's Semantic Differential, illustrating its use and value as a device for collecting and understanding customer perceptions of product offerings. Share your perspectives regarding the degree to which nonprofit organizations in your local community actively assess customer perceptions of their product offerings.

2. Select a local nonprofit organization and arrange to meet its top executive for the purpose of discussing the entity's techniques for the assessment of customer perceptions. Be sure to note any techniques that are employed, along with their frequency of deployment. Present Osgood, Suci, and Tannenbaum's Semantic Differential to the executive, and ask about variables deemed critical for measurement in his or her organization. Construct an instrument incorporating these variables and prepare a written account of insights gained from speaking with the organization's leader.

REFERENCE

Osgood, C. E., Suci, G. J., & Tannenbaum, P. H. (1957). *The measurement of meaning.* Urbana: University of Illinois Press.

PART V

Environmental Analysis and Competitive Assessment Tools

The PEST Analysis

LEARNING OBJECTIVES

After examining this chapter, readers will have the ability to:

- Understand that nonprofit entities exist in a large macroenvironment that consists of opportunities and threats with the potential to positively, neutrally, or negatively impact operations.
- Realize that environmental forces must actively be monitored and evaluated in an effort to best position nonprofit organizations to respond to such forces.
- Appreciate the value of the PEST Analysis as a tool for monitoring and evaluating the macroenvironment.

INTRODUCTION

Nonprofit entities exist in a large macroenvironment teeming with opportunities and threats capable of bolstering or destroying institutional progress. Although these environmental forces are beyond the control of those responsible for managing entities, it is essential for nonprofit executives to actively monitor and evaluate these elements in an effort to capitalize on opportunities and avoid or eliminate threats.

A useful tool for performing this evaluative task is known as the PEST Analysis. This analysis, illustrated in Figure 25-1, involves the assessment of a series of macroenvironmental variables (political, economic, social,

Political Forces	Economic Forces	Social Forces	Technological Forces
1. _____	1. _____	1. _____	1. _____
2. _____	2. _____	2. _____	2. _____
3. _____	3. _____	3. _____	3. _____
4. _____	4. _____	4. _____	4. _____
5. _____	5. _____	5. _____	5. _____
6. _____	6. _____	6. _____	6. _____
7. _____	7. _____	7. _____	7. _____
8. _____	8. _____	8. _____	8. _____
9. _____	9. _____	9. _____	9. _____
10. _____	10. _____	10. _____	10. _____

FIGURE 25-1 The PEST Analysis

and technological—hence the acronym *PEST*) that can potentially influ-ence organizations. Political, economic, social, and technological forces are defined as follows.

POLITICAL FORCES

Political forces involve all aspects associated with the legal and political framework of the environment. Quite obviously, political forces flow from those possessing such power, namely public officials (e.g., gover-nors, legislators, judges, mayors) and the vast administrative bureaucracies charged with implementing and overseeing their initiatives (e.g., com-merce departments, licensure boards, emergency preparedness councils, public works boards).

Political forces influence all establishments, regardless of industry or fo-cus, and they may serve as a benefit or detriment to given entities depend-ing on the nature of the particular force and its associated impact. Further, the political climate can change quite rapidly, motivated by newly elected regimes, alterations in political philosophy by those in power, or external factors that compel particular political responses. Nonprofit executives, of course, must be mindful of the political environment as it ultimately can enhance or constrain institutional operations.

ECONOMIC FORCES

Economic forces involve all aspects associated with the economy of a society, notably including factors related to economic health (e.g., inflation, unemployment, income). The economic climate exerts a powerful influence on both organizations and individuals. In weak economies, nonprofit entities might be forced to scale back or even eliminate product offerings. Rising costs might deter establishments from introducing new services or upgrading technologies. Expected and needed contributions from governmental entities and private donors might be scaled back or disappear entirely.

An environment of high unemployment might drive populations to rely on nonprofit entities more heavily, placing burdens on resources. Such an environment can destroy the demand for "want" items, such as trips to zoos, visits to museums, enrollment in graduate education programs, and the like. It can even curtail the demand for "need" items, such as food, water, clothing, medicine, electricity for the home, and so on. Alternatively, strong economies positively affect individuals and organizations in myriad ways.

SOCIAL FORCES

The social climate of a society impacts virtually every organization operating within the particular environment. Social forces include such aspects as the demographic composition and system of values and beliefs of a society. Demographic factors (e.g., age, gender, race, family size, education) heavily influence the product arrays provided by nonprofit entities. A youthful population, for example, will want and need goods and services that differ from those desired by an aging population. Differences in wants and needs will also be present between and among upper, middle, and lower class populations.

Values, too, highly influence the goods and services provided by establishments. Periods of altruism, for example, will likely result in the diversion of funds away from personal luxuries and toward worthy causes, which can be beneficial to nonprofit organizations. The same might be said of situations where natural disasters or other catastrophes have been experienced, prompting people to give more, both financially and of themselves personally, to help others. Values also dictate what particular experiences are offered by organizations. Periods where wholesome family entertainment is in vogue, for example, will place a premium on the delivery of experiences in keeping with such desires.

While values can be positive and uplifting to a society, they also can be negative and detrimental. Regions witnessing declining moral values, for example, can expect an increase in negative behaviors, such as drug use, domestic violence, and so forth, prompting nonprofit executives, where possible and applicable, to factor such environments into the way they go about addressing their target markets.

Regardless of the social forces at play in a given setting, nonprofit executives must be prepared to accurately assess prevailing characteristics and target their products properly in order to elicit desired results.

TECHNOLOGICAL FORCES

Technological forces significantly influence broad society in virtually every conceivable manner. Nonprofit entities have benefited from technological innovation both internally and externally, by incorporating various advancements into their operations (e.g., wireless communications, e-commerce solutions) and by incorporating the latest technologies into product offerings available to customers (e.g., advanced lifesaving interventions provided by ambulance companies, online courses offered by colleges and universities, state-of-the-art interactive displays provided by museums). Innovations are likely to become all the more spectacular with promising new developments on multiple scientific and technological frontiers, which will provide new opportunities for nonprofit entities to further realize gains, both for themselves and their clientele groups.

OPERATIONAL MATTERS

Formulating a PEST Analysis requires that nonprofit executives (1) construct the PEST diagram, as illustrated in Figure 25-1, (2) identify relevant macroenvironmental forces, and (3) describe how these forces are expected to impact given nonprofit entities. The resulting diagram is then analyzed to gain macroenvironmental insights.

Figure 25-2 presents a PEST Analysis that was developed for a convention and tourism bureau. This diagram clearly and concisely identifies relevant macroenvironmental forces. With this tool, the bureau can quickly assess macroenvironmental influences and formulate strategies and tactics to address pressing issues. Opportunities can be identified and exploited, while threats can be assessed and avoided or eliminated. The PEST Analysis allows nonprofit executives to proactively, rather than reactively, address macroenvironmental forces.

Importantly, the PEST Analysis should be conducted in an inclusive fashion where input from all organizational members involved in the development and management of associated goods and services is actively encouraged. The multiple perspectives offered by this extended group of individuals can greatly enhance resulting PEST Analyses.

It should be noted that the information derived from the PEST Analysis should ideally be combined with microenvironmental information (e.g., information regarding suppliers, competitors, customers). When this combination is accomplished, nonprofit executives possess a complete environmental assessment—invaluable information for planning marketing strategies and tactics.

Political Forces	Economic Forces	Social Forces	Technological Forces
State and local lawmakers introduce sales tax holidays ...*expected to*... Attract shoppers, including those from outside of the region	**Robust economy: rising income, low unemployment** ...*expected to*... Increase shopping activity; increase the ability of consumers to splurge on vacations; bolster general tourism to the area	**Growth of families with young children throughout the region** ...*expected to*... Increase the number of prospects for family vacations and other leisure opportunities	**Newly developed website featuring the latest technologies** ...*expected to*... Improve the manner in which the destination is presented to those considering the area for conventions, vacations, etc.
State lawmakers fund highway improvements facilitating access ...*expected to*... Increase tourism, courtesy of better transit routes into and out of the region	**Low fuel prices** ...*expected to*... Increase business and leisure travel to the area	**Growth in popularity of wholesome family entertainment** ...*expected to*... Increase demand for area attractions that constitute fun for the whole family, possibly bolstering tourism	**New digital advertising media introduced at regional airports** ...*expected to*... Improve bureau's ability to promote area attractions to those visiting the region

FIGURE 25-2 A Convention & Tourism Bureau's PEST Analysis

SUMMARY

With its external focus, the PEST Analysis provides nonprofit executives with a useful method for monitoring the macroenvironment. By routinely conducting this analysis, nonprofit executives can proactively respond to opportunities and threats that exist in the this environment, allowing their organizations the increased opportunity to achieve growth and prosperity.

EXERCISES

1. Define and comprehensively discuss the PEST Analysis, the four forces that the tool acts to monitor, and methodology associated with using this instrument. A diagram of the PEST Analysis should be included in your narrative. Share your thoughts regarding the tool's implications and uses in the nonprofit sector. Do you believe that modern nonprofit organizations are effectively monitoring their macroenvironments? Please justify your response.

2. Over the course of a one-month period, monitor national, regional, and local news sources, noting elements of the macroenvironment that have the potential to impact a local nonprofit entity of your choice. Then, develop a PEST Analysis incorporating these elements. Provide a brief narrative explaining overall discoveries and implications.

CHAPTER 26

The SWOT Analysis

LEARNING OBJECTIVES

After examining this chapter, readers will have the ability to:

- Realize the importance of routinely engaging in the systematic evaluation of product offerings in the marketplace.
- Understand the importance of identifying strengths, weaknesses, opportunities, and threats associated with nonprofit establishments and their product offerings.
- Appreciate the value of the SWOT Analysis as a tool for analyzing the state of affairs associated with nonprofit organizations and the various goods and services they provide to customers.

INTRODUCTION

Progressive nonprofit executives routinely engage in the systematic evaluation of their product offerings and associated target markets. For assistance in this evaluative process, they often rely on a tool known as the SWOT Analysis. Illustrated in Figure 26-1, the SWOT Analysis involves the identification of institutional strengths, weaknesses, opportunities, and threats—hence the acronym *SWOT*. As indicated in the diagram, strengths and weaknesses relate to internal environmental factors, while opportunities and threats pertain to external environmental factors. The SWOT Analysis is also known as a situation analysis because it focuses on an organization's state of affairs.

183

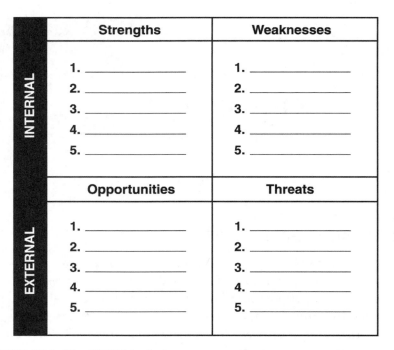

FIGURE 26-1 The SWOT Analysis

Although the SWOT Analysis has traditionally been used for institutional assessment purposes, it also serves as a highly effective tool for nonprofit executives when the focal point of the analysis is shifted from the organization to its product offerings. Instead of assessing the given entity (e.g., Grace Hospital), nonprofit executives analyze the strengths, weaknesses, opportunities, and threats of associated product offerings (e.g., Grace Hospital's labor-and-delivery unit, emergency department, clinic, wellness center). Strengths, weaknesses, opportunities, and threats are defined as follows.

STRENGTHS

Strengths are positive product and product-related attributes that facilitate exchange. Outstanding quality, excellent brand identity, rising market share, exceptional marketing management, superior research and development, world-class customer service, and patent protection are all

examples of product and product-related strengths. Through exploitation
of strengths, nonprofit executives can make great progress in the realization of marketing goals.

WEAKNESSES

Weaknesses are negative product and product-related attributes that
adversely impact exchange. Weaknesses might include poor customer
service, inconvenient access to offerings, inferior product quality,
outdated technology, declining market share, inadequate advertising
funds, and so on. Weaknesses undermine product performance and,
ultimately, exchange in the marketplace. Therefore, positive steps must
be taken to eliminate these negative attributes.

OPPORTUNITIES

Opportunities are external events and circumstances that have the potential
to positively impact products. Opportunities might include newly discovered product uses, substantial market growth, newly developed technologies,
anticipated favorable government legislation, and so on. Nonprofit executives must vigorously pursue and capitalize on opportunities to increase the
likelihood of institutional survival, growth, and prosperity.

THREATS

Threats are external events and circumstances that have the potential
to negatively impact products. Threats might include new competitors,
market attrition, anticipated adverse government legislation, changing
customer preferences, competitors equipped with superior technologies,
and superior substitute products. Nonprofit executives must endeavor to
develop strategies and tactics that will reduce or eliminate the potentially
detrimental impact of threats.

OPERATIONAL MATTERS

Formulating a SWOT Analysis requires that nonprofit executives
(1) construct the SWOT diagram, as illustrated in Figure 26-1,
(2) determine the particular product that will be evaluated, and

(3) identify associated strengths, weaknesses, opportunities, and threats. The resulting diagram is then analyzed to gain product insights.

Figure 26-2 presents a SWOT Analysis that was developed for a hospital's labor-and-delivery unit. This diagram illustrates the concise information portrayal offered by this simple, yet highly effective, marketing tool. With this tool, nonprofit executives can quickly assess internal and external product and product-related characteristics and influences—information that is essential for monitoring current performance and determining future strategic and tactical pursuits.

The SWOT Analysis can be used not only to assess the products held by evaluating entities but also to analyze the offerings held by competitors. This competitive analysis requires that nonprofit executives gain information regarding competitive offerings and then perform related SWOT Analyses. By using the SWOT Analysis in this fashion, organizations can gain many useful insights that can be of assistance in formulating marketing strategies and tactics.

	Strengths	Weaknesses
INTERNAL	Newly renovated unit Located in city's premier hospital Reputable physicians and nurses Large advertising budget Modern patient information system Greater capacity than competitors Best technology in community	Inadequate customer care delivered by some staff members High nurse employment turnover Inconvenient patient admit/discharge process Patient rooms not as elaborate as competitors
	Opportunities	**Threats**
EXTERNAL	Increasing number of women of childbearing age in the community Possible closure of one competing unit New and improved technologies available soon	Three competing units One new unit to open in 6 months Growing interest in midwifery Road construction hampering access to facility

FIGURE 26-2 A Labor & Delivery Unit's SWOT Analysis

While knowledge of the strengths, weaknesses, opportunities, and threats associated with particular products is most enlightening, non-profit executives must not neglect the value of performing the traditional, organization-focused SWOT Analysis. Goods and services are products of the organizations that produce and provide them. Coupling product-focused SWOT Analyses with organization-focused assessments will un-doubtedly provide a higher degree of insight into marketing operations than performing one of these assessments would provide.

It should be noted that while multiple SWOT Analyses are essentially required for nonprofit organizations with multiple product offerings, such detail may not be necessary in organizations with very few products. For example, small day care centers, medical clinics, specialty trade asso-ciations, and similar entities likely would need only one SWOT Analysis. Here, the organizations and their product offerings are virtually one and the same. A single SWOT Analysis would, therefore, be sufficient.

Importantly, the SWOT Analysis should be conducted in an inclusive fashion where input from all organizational members involved in the de-velopment and management of associated goods and services is actively encouraged. The multiple perspectives offered by this extended group of individuals can greatly enhance resulting SWOT Analyses.

SUMMARY

The SWOT Analysis provides a simple, convenient, and effective method for quickly assessing the internal and external factors associated with products and the nonprofit organizations that produce and provide them. Knowledge of this information allows nonprofit executives to formulate success-generat-ing strategies and tactics that will yield positive marketing outcomes.

EXERCISES

1. Provide a comprehensive overview of the SWOT Analysis, explaining its purpose, components, uses, and benefits, accompanied by an associated illustration. Be sure to indicate how the tool can be used not only for one's own product offerings, but also for the product offerings of competitors. Share your views regarding how this instrument can be used to effect success-generating strategies in the nonprofit sector.

2. Within your local marketplace, select a nonprofit entity and investigate its mission, product offerings, and so on using publicly available information, such as annual reports and the Internet. With this information, prepare a SWOT Analysis. Provide a narrative offering an overview of this assessment, your methods for its assembly, sources of information called upon for the analysis, and the resulting outlook for the nonprofit entity.

CHAPTER 27

Michael Porter's Five Forces Model

LEARNING OBJECTIVES

After examining this chapter, readers will have the ability to:

- Understand that competition and rivalry exist in the marketplace.
- Realize that nonprofit entities are required to possess a deep understanding of the competitive landscape to best position themselves for success.
- Recognize that competition is multidimensional, existing on multiple fronts, and that each front must be understood if marketing success is to be achieved.
- Realize that the nature of competition in any industry is based on five forces: existing competitors, potential entrants, substitutes, suppliers, and buyers.
- Appreciate the value of Michael Porter's Five Forces Model as a tool for understanding and addressing competition.

INTRODUCTION

The marketplace is characterized by competition and rivalry. Those entities that can successfully navigate the complex environment will be handsomely rewarded with satisfied target markets and resulting prosperity.

Successful navigation of this environment, of course, requires a deep understanding of marketplace competitors. All too often, however, nonprofit entities view their competitive environment in an overly narrow fashion, failing to acknowledge the true depth and breadth of competitive forces in the marketplace. Competition is multidimensional, and its vastness must be clearly understood if marketing success is to be achieved. The critical task of accurately identifying the competitive elements in a market is greatly facilitated by Michael Porter's Five Forces Model.

Illustrated in Figure 27-1, Porter's Five Forces Model provides useful insights into the multifaceted nature of competition. According to Porter, the nature of competition in any industry is based on five forces: existing competitors, potential entrants, substitutes, suppliers, and buyers. These forces are unique to each industry—and industry segment—and combine to determine the competitive intensity and ultimate potential of associated markets.

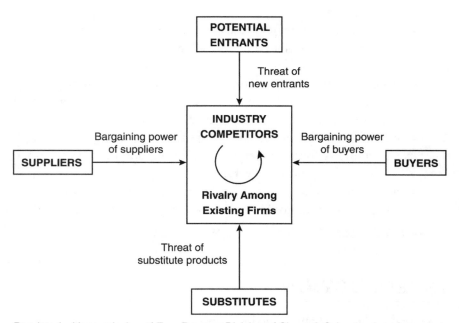

FIGURE 27-1 Porter's Five Forces Model

EXISTING COMPETITORS

Existing competitors are the most obvious competitive force, jockeying for position through new product development, innovative promotional campaigns, and so on. Rivalry among existing competitors is especially intense when competitors are numerous and fairly equivalent in terms of size and power; when exit barriers are high; and when industry growth is slow, resulting in struggles for market share. These characteristics are often observed in the nonprofit marketplace, illustrating the intense rivalry that can be found in this sector.

POTENTIAL ENTRANTS

Entities that might potentially enter the market represent significant threats to existing competitors. New entrants bring new capacity and resources to the market along with desires for market share. The magnitude of the threat posed by new entrants is largely based on the particular barriers to entry that exist. Typical examples of entry barriers include capital requirements, proprietary product differences, government policy, and the market dominance and brand identity of existing competitors. Significant entry barriers yield significant protection from the threat of new entrants, while few barriers increase the competitive nature of the market. Certificates of need possessed by hospitals, for example, are illustrative of mechanisms that provide substantial protection for their holders. Similarly, governmental restrictions on the type and number of specialized academic degree programs within given regions insulate the institutions that are actually offering those degrees from the threat of competition.

SUBSTITUTES

Substitutes are products that differ from particular offerings but largely, and sometimes completely, fill equivalent wants and needs. As a result, substitute offerings can greatly impact the performance of nonprofit entities and even threaten their very existence. A trip to the movies could be viewed as a substitute for a visit to a museum. Travel via private car could be viewed as a substitute for travel via mass transit. The seriousness of the threat of substitutes is predominantly based on their performance and price characteristics. Substitutes that offer equal or better performance pose significant threats, especially when price advantages exist.

SUPPLIERS

Suppliers provide the components necessary for nonprofit organizations to offer goods and services to their customers. Supplies constitute anything and everything necessary for an entity to offer its products to target audiences. Without these "raw materials," nonprofit entities could not function. This dependence on suppliers poses a significant threat to nonprofit entities. Suppliers can raise their prices, lower the quality of the components that they provide, or simply go out of business—all situations that can yield potentially devastating effects. Suppliers are particularly powerful if they are few in number, if few substitutes exist, and if entities are not key customers.

BUYERS

Porter's term *buyers* is equivalent to the term *customers*, which is better suited for the nonprofit marketplace. Quite obviously, customers possess significant bargaining power over nonprofit entities because their patronage ultimately determines institutional survival, growth, and prosperity. The array of customers in the nonprofit marketplace is quite varied, including patrons of museums, patients in hospital beds, students at elementary schools, recipients of disaster relief services, and even the various governmental agencies and other third-party payer entities that pay for services on behalf of constituents. Without customers, operations cease. For this reason, nonprofit executives must ensure that all marketing efforts are customer focused. Importantly, they must strive to accurately assess the wants and needs of customers and serve them in a manner that will meet and exceed their expectations.

OPERATIONAL MATTERS

Porter's Five Forces Model is highly useful in that it clearly illustrates the multidimensional nature of marketplace competition. Its use, however, can be extended through the assembly and completion of a Five Forces

Worksheet. Nonprofit executives simply (1) identify the product offering to be evaluated, (2) construct the Five Forces Worksheet, as illustrated in Figure 27-2, (3) identify existing competitors, potential entrants, substitutes, suppliers, and buyers, and (4) place the identified current and potential competitors on the diagram accordingly. When completed, the Five Forces Worksheet identifies all five competitive forces that entities currently face or could potentially face, as illustrated in Figure 27-3. This particular diagram can be even more valuable if competitors are identified by name in the schematic. Completion of this device yields considerable insights into the current and future competitive marketplace and hence serves as an essential marketing planning tool.

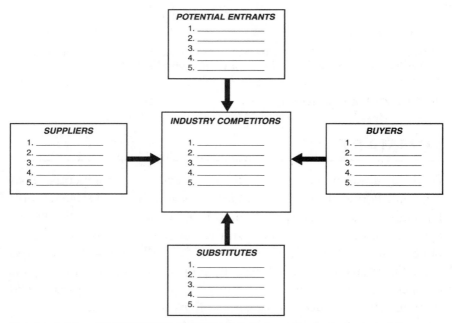

FIGURE 27-2 A Five Forces Worksheet

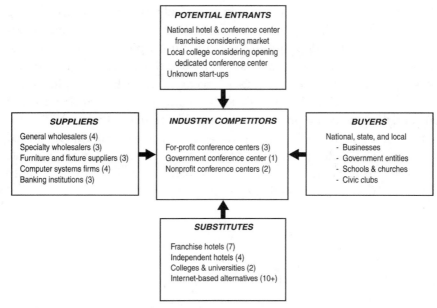

FIGURE 27-3 A Conference Center's Five Forces Worksheet

SUMMARY

By clearly illustrating the true depth and breadth of the competitive environment, Porter's Five Forces Model serves as an indispensable resource for nonprofit executives. With this information, they can establish strategic and tactical priorities and position their organizations to capitalize on opportunities and avoid or eliminate threats. Ideally, nonprofit executives will address each of the five forces. By properly addressing the complete competitive environment, nonprofit executives are better prepared to meet and exceed related performance objectives.

EXERCISES

1. Define and comprehensively discuss Michael Porter's Five Forces Model, providing insights regarding its uses, features, methods of interpretation, and value, accompanied by an appropriate

illustration. Be sure to include in your discussion an overview of the instrument's importance as a strategic marketing device in the nonprofit sector.

2. Select a nonprofit entity of your choice for placement in your local market and assign the hypothetical establishment an appropriate brand name. Consult a variety of information sources (e.g., telephone directories, the Internet, industry databases) in an effort to identify entities occupying associated categories of competition listed in Michael Porter's Five Forces Model, preparing an appropriate illustration accordingly. Based on your Five Forces Model, what have you learned about the depth and breadth of competition in the marketplace?

REFERENCE

Porter, M. E. (1998). *Competitive strategy: Techniques for analyzing industries and competitors*. New York, NY: The Free Press.

CHAPTER 28

Lehmann and Winer's Levels of Competition Model

LEARNING OBJECTIVES

After examining this chapter, readers will have the ability to:

- Recognize that every competitor represents a potential threat to the operations of nonprofit establishments.
- Understand that the actions of rivals must be closely monitored to proactively address developing issues, events, and circumstances.
- Recognize that nonprofit executives often define their competitive field too narrowly, failing to realize the true extent of competition in the marketplace.
- Appreciate the value afforded by Lehmann and Winer's Levels of Competition Model as an instrument for accurately identifying and understanding competition.

INTRODUCTION

Progressive nonprofit executives understand that it is essential to accurately identify and assess their competition because every competitor represents a threat. Although nonprofit executives cannot control their competitors, they can closely monitor the actions of rivals and proactively address developing issues. When nonprofit executives fail to identify competitors, they inadvertently afford the unidentified rivals with the strategic advantage of operational secrecy. This gives competitors the element of surprise and, along with it, valuable time to secure market share.

Possibly the most common competitive assessment error committed by nonprofit executives is that of defining the competitive field too narrowly. To aid in understanding the true extent of the competitive environment, Donald Lehmann and Russell Winer developed a diagram that depicts levels of market competition.

Illustrated in Figure 28-1, Lehmann and Winer's Levels of Competition Model identifies four competitive levels—product form, product category, generic, and budget—that are depicted by four concentric circles that surround the product under evaluation. Competitive offerings are placed on the diagram based on how they compare to the product under evaluation. Competitive products that occupy inner levels of the diagram are more comparable to the product under evaluation than those that occupy outer levels. The four competitive levels are defined as follows.

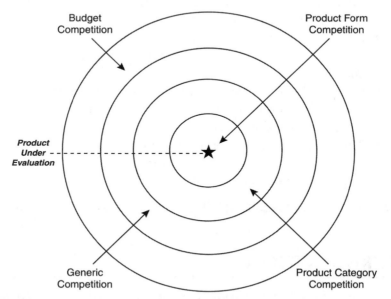

FIGURE 28-1 Lehmann & Winer's Levels of Competition Model

PRODUCT FORM COMPETITION

Product form competition is the narrowest view that can be taken of competition. Identified by the innermost circle on the Levels of Competition Model, product form competition includes all competitive products that have roughly equivalent product features and compete in the same market segments. At this level, competitive entities include direct, head-to-head rivals that offer similar goods and services and compete for the same "turf."

PRODUCT CATEGORY COMPETITION

The level just beyond product form competition is known as product category competition. Here, competition expands to include all competitive products that possess similar features, regardless of the market segments targeted. Competition at this level represents what organization leaders have traditionally viewed as their competitive set.

GENERIC COMPETITION

The third level of competition is known as generic competition. Generic competition includes all competing products that, although unrelated to given product offerings, fill equivalent wants and needs. Whereas product form and product category levels are inward focused (i.e., focused on products similar to those produced and provided by given entities), generic competition is outward focused (i.e., focused on potential alternatives or substitutes for associated product offerings). Nonprofit executives wishing to capitalize on opportunities and avoid threats must be certain that their view of competition includes the generic level. Such a focus will ensure that nonprofit executives avoid what Theodore Levitt termed *marketing myopia*—a detrimental practice where entities define their operations too narrowly.

BUDGET COMPETITION

Budget competition, the outermost level of competition, involves all products that compete for the same customer dollar. Budget competition represents the broadest view of competition. Although budget competition is useful from a conceptual perspective, it is of very little strategic value because the number of potential competitive offerings is so immense.

OPERATIONAL MATTERS

To assess product competition using Lehmann and Winer's Levels of Competition Model, nonprofit executives simply (1) identify the product offering to be evaluated, (2) construct the Levels of Competition diagram, as illustrated in Figure 28-1, (3) identify product form, product category, generic, and budget competitors, and (4) place the identified competitors on the diagram accordingly. The resulting Levels of Competition diagram is then analyzed to gain insights into product competition.

Figure 28-2 presents a Levels of Competition Model that was developed for an urban, nonprofit medical center that primarily serves a mixture of insured and uninsured populations. At the product form level, the medical center would view its competition as other local medical centers that provide the same services to the same customer populations. The product category level represents a broadened competitive scope that would include all medical centers in the marketplace, regardless of the clientele served. Here, the medical center would include facilities that primarily serve insured customers, along with all other medical centers in the marketplace, regardless of their particular target markets.

At the generic level, the competitive scope increases significantly to include facilities that address similar wants and needs. Here, the medical center would add area clinics, health departments, and other health service providers to its competitive framework. Although these entities do not directly compete with the medical center, they do offer alternatives in many clinical areas for prospective customers.

Lastly, budget competition could be anything and everything, related or not, that might divert customer resources away from the medical center. An individual might, for example, forgo an elective medical procedure—or even one that is medically necessary—to pay for his or her child's college tuition, to take a vacation, to buy a new car, to purchase furniture, and so on.

Figure 28-3 presents a Levels of Competition Model that was developed for a nonprofit golf course. At the product form level, the golf course would view its competition as other nonprofit and public golf courses serving the broad population. At the product category level, the

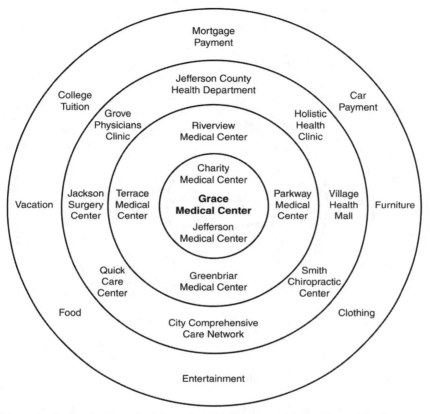

Constructed using design methodologies in Lehmann, Donald R., and Russell S. Winer. 2005. Analysis for marketing planning. 6th ed. New York: McGraw-Hill.

FIGURE 28-2 A Medical Center's Levels of Competition Model

golf course would view its competition as all area golf courses, regardless of ownership and clientele served. Here, for example, local private golf courses would be added.

At the generic level, the competitive scope increases to include sports and recreation entities that address similar wants and needs, namely the enjoyment of fitness-related activities. Here, the golf course would add area tennis clubs, yacht clubs, fitness centers, and other sports and recreation service providers to its competitive framework. All of these entities provide sports and recreation alternatives for prospective customers. Lastly, budget competition would include anything that would compete

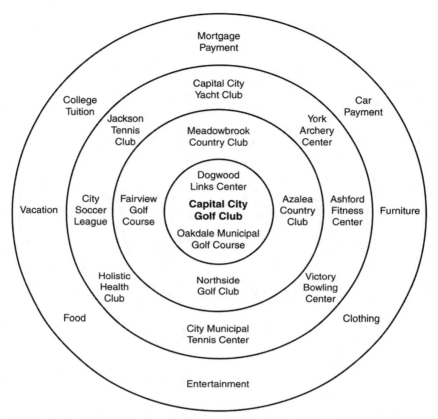

Constructed using design methodologies in Lehmann, Donald R., and Russell S. Winer. 2005. Analysis for marketing planning. 6th ed. New York: McGraw-Hill.

FIGURE 28-3 A Golf Course's Levels of Competition Model

for the golf recreation dollars of customers: a down payment on a house, a computer, clothing, jewelry, and so on.

It is important to remember that in the nonprofit marketplace, some product offerings do not have appropriate substitutes. A hospital emergency department would certainly compete with other area emergency departments, potentially at both the product form and product category levels. However, as providers of potentially lifesaving services for the ill and injured, they stand alone and, as a result, do not have any competition of note at the generic level. Given that patients receiving such services are fighting for their lives, budget competition would also be of little concern to any emergency department. The same ultranarrow competitive field applies to those nonprofit entities that are the providers of last resort for given populations. Soup kitchens, homeless shelters, and other welfare-minded entities may in fact be the only ones of their kind in their area. Quite obviously, certain nonprofit entities possess unique, and in some cases very limited, competitive fronts.

It is also important to note that the Levels of Competition Model does not assess the threat potential forwarded by competitive elements. For example, in Figure 28-3, it might be very likely that a generic competitor, such as a municipal tennis center, would pose more of a threat to the golf course under evaluation than a product category competitor, such as a private golf course. Instead, the model identifies competitive elements based on their characteristics in relation to the product under evaluation. It categorizes competition by *type* of competitor, which does not necessarily equate with threat intensity. Given this, it might be useful to indicate on the Levels of Competition diagram those offerings, regardless of their competitive level, that are believed to pose the most significant threat to the product under evaluation. This information greatly assists nonprofit executives in determining strategic and tactical priorities, particularly in the area of product promotion.

SUMMARY

Given the dangers associated with defining the competitive field too narrowly, nonprofit executives must diligently seek to identify all current and potential rivals in the market. Lehmann and Winer's Levels of Competition Model serves as a useful guide for nonprofit executives to consult in this pursuit, reminding them of the true extent of competitive elements in the marketplace.

EXERCISES

1. Provide a detailed overview of Lehmann and Winer's Levels of Competition Model, noting facets regarding its purpose, use, implementation, and value in nonprofit organizations. Preface your work by discussing the competitive nature of the nonprofit sector and the need for monitoring the activities of rivals. Be sure to share your perspectives regarding the degree to which modern nonprofit organizations actively and accurately define their competitive fields.

2. Within your local marketplace, identify a nonprofit product offering. Then, study the offering, seeking information on its features and benefits, position in the marketplace, and competitive field. Based on this assessment, construct a Levels of Competition Model for the product, identifying product form, product category, generic, and budget competitors. Be sure to indicate on the diagram those offerings that are believed to pose the most significant threat to the product under evaluation. Provide a narrative explaining your illustration.

REFERENCES

Lehmann, D. R., & Winer, R. S. (2005). *Analysis for marketing planning* (6th ed.). New York, NY: McGraw-Hill.

Levitt, T. (1960, July/August). Marketing myopia. *Harvard Business Review, 38,* 45–56.

CHAPTER 29

Mintzberg and Van der Heyden's Organigraph

> **LEARNING OBJECTIVES**
>
> *After examining this chapter, readers will have the ability to:*
> - Realize that progressive nonprofit executives must possess an intuitive knowledge of their organizations, product offerings, sought markets, and associated environmental relationships.
> - Recognize that visualizing inter- and intraorganizational relationships increases the understanding of such relationships, permitting nonprofit executives to formulate productive strategies.
> - Appreciate the value afforded by Mintzberg and Van der Heyden's Organigraph as a tool for shedding light on the inter- and intraorganizational relationships of nonprofit institutions.

INTRODUCTION

Progressive nonprofit executives clearly understand that to achieve marketing success, they must possess an intricate knowledge of their organizations, the products offered, the markets sought, and associated environmental relationships. With such knowledge, nonprofit executives are able to formulate productive strategies that yield positive marketing results.

Gaining this extensive insight into inter- and intraorganizational relationships, however, is not a simple activity because these facets are typically quite complex. Achieving this understanding can be hastened, however, by assembling and analyzing an Organigraph, an evaluative tool developed by Henry Mintzberg and Ludo Van der Heyden.

In essence, an Organigraph is a diagram that depicts the activities and operations of organizations. Mintzberg and Van der Heyden developed the Organigraph to shed light on the often complex inter- and intraorganizational relationships of institutions—a feat that the traditional organizational chart cannot accomplish. The Organigraph derives its name from the word *organigramme*, the French term for organizational chart.

Rather than using the series of boxes and lines that are common in organizational charts, the Organigraph uses a series of shapes to illustrate the actual relationships that exist inside and outside of organizations. This feature increases the level of detail that can be incorporated into these diagrams.

Although the construction and use of Organigraphs is typically associated with strategic management, these tools also have marketing applications. By depicting inter- and intraorganizational relationships, most notably those dealing with suppliers and target markets, Organigraphs can be quite helpful to nonprofit executives seeking an overall view of their entities and associated interrelationships, many of which directly impact marketing.

CONSTRUCTING AN ORGANIGRAPH

Constructing an Organigraph requires imagination. Unlike organizational charts, which have strict rules governing their assembly, Organigraphs do not possess such guidelines. To construct an Organigraph, nonprofit executives must (1) think about their organizations, the products offered, the markets sought, and associated environmental relationships, and (2) map this vision using a series of shapes that accurately illustrates associated activities and operations.

As illustrated in Figure 29-1, Organigraphs are typically assembled using some combination of four primary components: sets, chains, hubs, and webs. A set indicates an independent relationship, a chain indicates the progressive development or assembly of something, a hub indicates a coordinating center that links activities, and a web indicates a series of nodes depicting relationships among components that do not possess a coordinating center. Other shapes can, of course, be used to assemble Organigraphs, provided that the shapes accurately convey relationships.

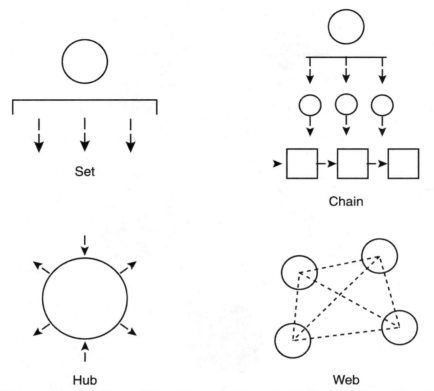

FIGURE 29-1 Common Components of Organigraphs

OPERATIONAL MATTERS

Figure 29-2 illustrates an Organigraph that was constructed for a workforce development center. Quite noticeably, the Organigraph is shaped as a web, indicating the presence of relationships among the center's four departments: placement services, resume development, aptitude testing, and career counseling.

As indicated in the diagram, each of these departments interacts with one another but operates in a largely autonomous fashion in the course of serving clients. These departments, for example, independently schedule client appointments, coordinate internal activities, and manage client account

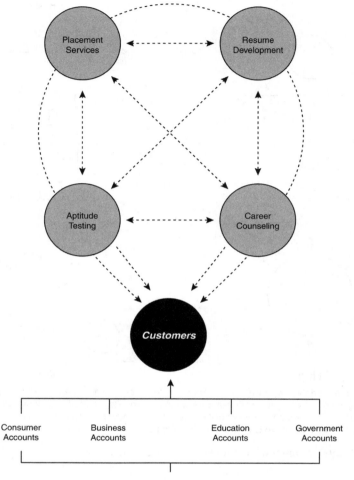

Constructed using design methodologies in Mintzberg, Henry, and Ludo Van der Heyden. 1999. Organigraphs: Drawing how companies really work. Harvard Business Review (September–October): 87–94.

FIGURE 29-2 A Workforce Development Center's Organigraph

information. Also of note in the Organigraph is the depiction of the center's customer base, identified by customer type and geographic location.

If desired, the center could create a more detailed Organigraph that illustrates suppliers, competitors, internal support departments (e.g., accounting, human resources), and so on. With this additional detail, the Organigraph easily becomes a strategic tool that possesses value for all administrative units within the entity.

Figure 29-3 depicts an Organigraph that was constructed for a food bank. This diagram uses the hub shape to clearly and concisely illustrate the coordinating role of the agency's central office and warehouse, which

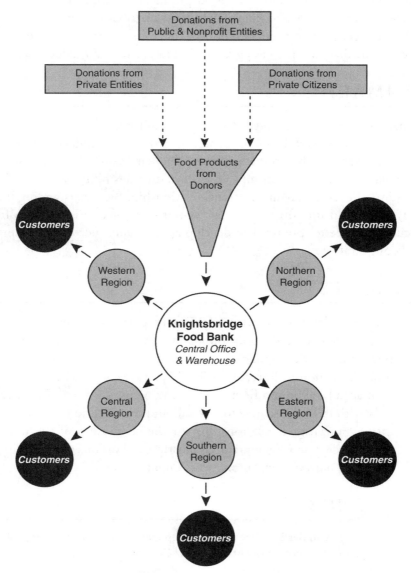

Constructed using design methodologies in Mintzberg, Henry, and Ludo Van der Heyden. 1999. Organigraphs: Drawing how companies really work. Harvard Business Review (September–October): 87–94.

FIGURE 29-3 A Food Bank's Organigraph

distributes food products and provides direction to its five regions that ultimately deliver nutritional items to clients. In illustrating the supplier role in this diagram, the food bank used a funnel shape to indicate the collection of multiple elements—food products from donors—that are directed into the entity and then routed to its distribution centers located in different geographic regions. If desired, of course, more detail could be added to the diagram, increasing its value and use within the food bank.

SUMMARY

Mintzberg and Van der Heyden's Organigraph provides nonprofit executives with a powerful tool for achieving a thorough understanding of their organizations, the products offered, the markets sought, and associated environmental relationships. The diagram's flexibility allows the illustration of virtually any institutional relationship. By understanding the many inter- and intraorganizational relationships of entities, nonprofit executives are better prepared to develop appropriate, success-generating marketing strategies.

EXERCISES

1. Prepare a detailed overview of Mintzberg and Van der Heyden's Organigraph, describing its foundations, uses, methods of construction, and practical applications. What are the implications of this tool for the nonprofit sector? Why do you view this to be the case?
2. Contact a local nonprofit entity and arrange an informational interview with its top executive to learn about the institution's inter- and intraorganizational relationships. At the conclusion of the interview, develop an Organigraph to illustrate the various relationships. Provide a narrative explaining your Organigraph.

REFERENCE

Mintzberg, H., & Van der Heyden, L. (1999, September/October). Organigraphs: Drawing how companies really work. *Harvard Business Review, 77*, 87–94.

PART VI

Marketing Management, Strategy, and Planning Tools

CHAPTER 30

John Fortenberry's CMC (Core Marketing Concerns) Model

LEARNING OBJECTIVES

After examining this chapter, readers will have the ability to:

- Realize the important role of marketing, arguably serving as the most critical management responsibility associated with the pursuit and realization of growth and prosperity.
- Understand the proper definition of marketing, as well as the true depth and breadth of the discipline.
- Recognize that a successful marketing department must address the discipline in its entirety in order to realize the full power of marketing.
- See the value of Fortenberry's CMC (Core Marketing Concerns) Model as an aid in designing marketing departments that are structured to comprehensively address the discipline and deliver superior performance.

INTRODUCTION

Marketing is defined in many different ways by many different people and, sadly, many of these definitions are inaccurate. Perhaps the most frequently observed inaccuracy pertains to defining marketing in an overly narrow fashion, typically equating it as being one and the same with marketing communications, or, even more narrowly, advertising. Embracing a definition that portrays marketing in a highly limited fashion will yield marketing operations that are just as limited, diminishing the potential of given marketing departments.

Properly defined, marketing is a management process that involves the assessment of customer wants and needs, and the performance of all activities associated with the development, pricing, provision, and promotion of product solutions that satisfy those wants and needs. This particular definition draws attention to the many facets of marketing, which go well beyond advertising and other forms of marketing communication.

While a proper definition aids in understanding the depth and breadth of the discipline, it provides little direction as to how to go about designing, structuring, and directing the efforts of marketing operations in organizations. Of course, comprehensive investigations in voluminous marketing textbooks offer suggestions, but typically, the end result is something overly complex with limited practical value. At the simplest possible descriptive level, what are the primary concerns that an organization's marketing department must address and what particular foundation is required to ensure success in addressing these concerns? An answer to such would serve to help new organizations establish productive marketing departments and remind existing marketing departments of core priorities. Importantly, such a framework also would be most helpful in conveying the essence of marketing to those unfamiliar with the discipline's important role in organizations.

In an effort to provide associated guidance, John Fortenberry developed the Core Marketing Concerns (CMC) Model. According to Fortenberry, a complete and successful marketing system in an organization requires the establishment of a performance-oriented marketing infrastructure that adequately addresses three prevailing concerns: product concerns, communications concerns, and research concerns. Fortenberry originally devised the model to help students more quickly grasp the discipline of marketing; however, he discovered that it proved to be quite useful for informing both new and seasoned executives alike of a marketing department's chief concerns and the requisite infrastructure for productively addressing those concerns.

As illustrated in Figure 30-1, Fortenberry's CMC Model consists of a large circle, representing the marketing infrastructure of an organization,

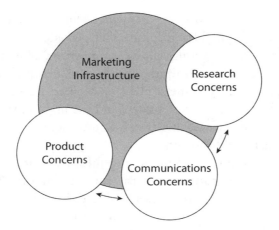

FIGURE 30-1 Fortenberry's Core Marketing Concerns (CMC) Model

which serves as the foundation for three smaller circles, representing each of the core marketing concerns. Importantly, the three smaller circles are positioned in a manner extending beyond the rim of the larger circle, indicating interdepartmental influence. The arrows in the diagram indicate the existence of interrelationships between and among the core marketing concerns. Although each concern is discussed independently herein, quite obviously, associated linkages are highly pronounced. The model's elements are explained as follows.

THE MARKETING INFRASTRUCTURE

The marketing infrastructure element of Fortenberry's CMC Model essentially refers to the foundational design and composition of an organization's marketing department. Without an appropriate and effective infrastructure, marketing pursuits will suffer weaknesses and never reach their full potential. The backbone of the marketing infrastructure rests with its personnel, each of whom must be well trained, highly motivated by challenges, and profoundly capable of viewing the world through the eyes of others. Marketing staff members must understand the importance of marketing not only to outside parties (i.e., external marketing), but also to internal parties (i.e., internal marketing), as each employee of an organization plays a critical role in marketing success and, as such, must possess a marketing mindset.

Indeed, a proper marketing infrastructure requires the establishment and maintenance of a marketing culture that pervades the entire organization. Specifically, a marketing culture is one where all employees consciously view their given organizations and associated product offerings from the perspective of customers. Here, employees, regardless of job title, pay grade, or education level, understand the importance of thinking *first* of customers. In essence, they become customer service ambassadors for their particular establishments.

Importantly, a well-devised marketing infrastructure will contain a marketing department that possesses the complete and total support of the top leaders of the organization. These leaders must understand the critical role that marketing plays in their given establishment and, in turn, facilitate the department's efforts and initiatives to deliver excellence throughout its many endeavors. Prudent incentives, available to all employees, should be instituted, with rewards being forwarded to those whose behaviors positively promote the organization and its product offerings.

A solid marketing infrastructure provides a firm administrative foundation, permitting marketing departments to direct their unequivocal attention to the core concerns of the discipline. With such a foundation in place, these prevailing concerns can be addressed fully and productively.

PRODUCT CONCERNS

The product concerns component of the CMC Model pertains to every imaginable aspect associated with the offerings of a given establishment. Every product, whether it is a good or a service, ultimately consists of a bundle of attributes; these attributes must be formulated, managed, and, when necessary, updated to ensure that they appeal to target audiences.

While obvious product-related activities of concern to marketing departments include the management of existing offerings and the development of new ones, associated responsibilities go well beyond such. Relevant additional concerns include the manner in which products are priced, the courtesy of personnel in addressing customer inquiries, the quality of the servicescapes in which products are presented, the availability of product offerings at times and places that customers find appealing, and so on. Negative product attributes counter positive ones, so efforts must be taken to elevate each product and product-related facet to its highest level, lifting the collective value of given goods and services as seen through the eyes of customers.

Effective marketing departments take product-related responsibilities very seriously. Their personnel actively network with other organizational departments to ensure that the entire institution understands the value that all organizational members play in producing and providing associated goods and services. Given that control over these external departments does not rest with marketing executives, yet marketing success is dependent on organizations in their entirety, skill at diplomacy is a worthwhile quality for those serving in marketing roles.

COMMUNICATIONS CONCERNS

The communications concerns component of the CMC Model entails anything and everything that is used to communicate with external parties, with most of the attention being placed on reaching and attracting target audiences. Without appropriate and effective marketing communications, target audiences will not be informed of given product offerings, regardless of how brilliant the associated goods and services might be. Quite obviously, product excellence alone is not enough for marketing success. Communications excellence also is required.

The communications concerns component is the one that is most traditionally associated with marketing, likely because it is the most visible of marketing endeavors since such initiatives are directed toward the outside world, visible for all to see. Marketing communications begins with branding, which involves the application of names, symbols, logos, and other identifiers to products in an effort to convey desired images to target audiences and assist in product differentiation. Then, organizations call on the promotions mix—the five major categories of communication, namely, advertising, personal selling, sales promotion, public relations, and direct marketing—to engage target markets. Formulation of this mix, which also is referred to as the communications mix, is based on determining the most appropriate and effective methods for reaching target audiences, something typically involving experimentation (i.e., trial and error).

Marketing departments serve as in-house communications experts, working on behalf of their organizations to initiate a dialogue with target audiences in an effort to attract and retain their patronage. These departments must be staffed by skilled individuals who possess a profound understanding of the communications options at their disposal, along with the ability to design effective marketing communications campaigns, making adjustments as necessary to best reach and attract defined audiences.

RESEARCH CONCERNS

The final component of the CMC Model pertains to research concerns. This particular component focuses on the acquisition and dissemination of marketing intelligence, with a heavy emphasis being on monitoring the environment, observing business metrics, and designing and implementing mechanisms permitting the measurement of marketing performance.

Typical marketing research endeavors include administering customer satisfaction surveys, conducting focus groups to determine the product preferences of target markets, supervising mystery shopping initiatives to monitor the customer service behaviors of employees, surveying customers to ascertain whether they noticed certain marketing communications, monitoring sales volume and other business metrics in the context of marketing communications to ascertain impact, and the supervision of systems for formally monitoring the external environment.

The research concerns component is perhaps the most neglected of the three elements in the CMC Model, likely due to the complexities associated with such endeavors. However, without a developed marketing research program, marketing departments are conducting operations in an uninformed fashion, lacking a detailed understanding of virtually every initiative for which they are responsible.

Only sound marketing research can answer questions such as the following: Which of the three media used in an advertising campaign delivered the most value? What will our customers think about an anticipated product modification? How can we best communicate a new product to our target markets? What strategies are our competitors using to attract customers? Through such research, knowledge emerges that improves marketing performance and, ultimately, institutional growth and prosperity.

SUMMARY

Fortenberry's CMC Model provides guidance in the assembly of marketing departments that are designed and structured to comprehensively address the discipline and deliver superior performance. By directing attention to the three prevailing concerns of marketing departments—product concerns, communications concerns, and research concerns—and emphasizing the establishment of a performance-oriented marketing infrastructure, organizations are prepared to realize the full potential of the discipline of marketing.

EXERCISES

1. Define and comprehensively discuss Fortenberry's CMC Model, its elements, and its value as an instrument for the assembly of progressive marketing departments. A diagram of the CMC Model should be included to add value to your narrative. Do you believe nonprofit institutions routinely structure their marketing operations in accordance with this model? Why do you believe this to be the case?

2. Contact a local nonprofit entity and arrange an informational interview with its top executive to gain insights into the design and operation of the organization's marketing system. At the conclusion of the interview, evaluate the establishment's marketing system using Fortenberry's CMC Model. Report your findings in detail.

Leonard Berry's Success Sustainability Model

INTRODUCTION

Administrative excellence does not arise out of luck or chance, but rather through the development and implementation of appropriate institutional systems that guide entities to prosperity. Numerous systems must be incorporated, but possibly none is as important as the underlying array of principles embraced by nonprofit organizations. The composition of these principles ultimately determines the potential of nonprofit entities to achieve and sustain success.

To understand the prerequisites for sustained operational excellence, nonprofit executives often refer to Leonard Berry's Success Sustainability Model, which was developed from Berry's research inquiries into the practices of top-performing service organizations.

Illustrated in Figure 31-1, Berry's Success Sustainability Model is depicted as a circular diagram containing nine boxes that denote drivers of excellence. Eight of these drivers—strategic focus, executional excellence, control of destiny, trust-based relationships, investment in employee success, acting small, brand cultivation, and generosity—occupy boxes that encompass the perimeter of the diagram, each extending from the primary driver (i.e., values-driven leadership) situated in the center of

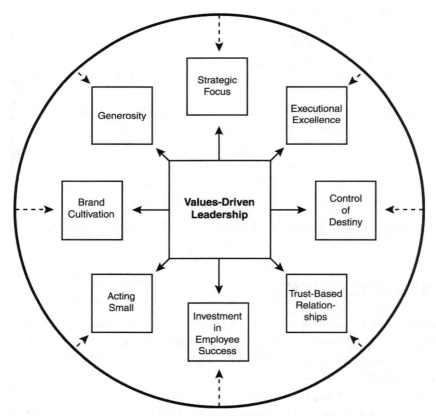

FIGURE 31-1 Berry's Success Sustainability Model

the diagram. Arrows drawn with solid lines denote primary relationships, while those drawn with dotted lines indicate interrelationships among success drivers. The nine drivers of excellence are defined as follows.

VALUES-DRIVEN LEADERSHIP

Values-driven leadership serves as the foundation of all other drivers of excellence. Values represent the core beliefs held by organizations. If these values are not strong, sustainable success cannot be achieved. Importantly, nonprofit entities seeking sustained success must possess seven core values: excellence (i.e., striving for high performance in all areas), innovation (i.e., striving to make current offerings better), joy (i.e., working to uplift the human spirit and celebrate achievement), teamwork (i.e., collaborating to achieve common goals), respect (i.e., concern for employees, customers, suppliers, and others), integrity (i.e., conducting operations in an ethical fashion), and social profit (i.e., giving back to the community).

These values must actively be communicated by leaders, demonstrated through value-laden actions, and cultivated to achieve excellence. By embracing these values, nonprofit organizations establish solid institutional foundations that foster excellence.

STRATEGIC FOCUS

Nonprofit organizations seeking sustained success must formulate strategies that embody their values. Specifically, the formulation of these strategies requires that entities clearly define their operations and develop specialized systems of activities to implement their missions. Strategies should reflect the dynamic and innovative nature of nonprofit entities. Nonprofit organizations must strive to ensure that their strategies remain mission focused because deviations hamper the attainment of excellence.

A hospital, for example, that embraces a mission of providing comprehensive services to a rural population must formulate an array of strategies that focuses exclusively on the delivery of quality health services to its rural target market. If the hospital deviates from its mission by formulating divergent strategies that target, say, urban populations, the establishment has obviously lost sight of its mission and will ultimately suffer the perils associated with a failed strategic focus, notably institutional decline and, possibly, failure.

EXECUTIONAL EXCELLENCE

Not only must nonprofit organizations formulate well-planned strategies, but they also must ensure that these strategies are appropriately and successfully executed through sound tactics. Execution is as important as the strategy itself, and progressive nonprofit entities place a significant emphasis on excellence in this area. Tactical pursuits must flow directly from the strategies embraced by nonprofit entities for excellence to be achieved. Through well-executed tactics, strategic goals and objectives are accomplished, thus fulfilling associated missions. The best developed missions and accompanying strategies are pointless if they are not executed appropriately through sound tactics, hence the importance of excellence in this area.

CONTROL OF DESTINY

Control of destiny is largely an attitudinal mindset, which holds that by taking appropriate actions, establishments can control the future. Such actions taken by nonprofit entities in an effort to control their destiny might include the continuous enhancement of service-delivery technologies, the recruitment and retention of highly qualified personnel, the delivery of products that possess significant value, and the establishment of world-class customer service.

Nonprofit entities that possess a control-of-destiny mindset are prepared to positively address the rigorous environment and its associated challenges. This positive mindset undoubtedly motivates these organizations to take success-generating actions that enhance prosperity.

TRUST-BASED RELATIONSHIPS

Nonprofit entities cannot attain success without conducting all operations in a genuine fashion. This type of conduct involves honoring obligations and commitments, treating all parties fairly and respectfully, maintaining high ethical standards, and so on. When a credit counseling agency takes steps to ensure that its employees address clients in a courteous manner, it establishes trust with its customer base. When a trade association meets financial obligations with its vendors in a timely fashion, it establishes trust with these various suppliers. When a community college takes steps to ensure that the latest technologies are incorporated into its classrooms, it establishes trust with its student population. When a medical center ensures that patient confidentiality is maintained, it establishes trust with its patient population. Trust allows the formation of lasting, commitment-laden relationships with customers, employees, suppliers, and communities.

INVESTMENT IN EMPLOYEE SUCCESS

A talented labor force represents a key source of competitive advantage. The ability to recruit and retain the best employees requires an investment in their professional growth and development that indirectly represents an investment in the organizations that sponsor such assistance. The environment is continuously changing, requiring that nonprofit entities ensure that their employees, both administrative and technical, possess the tools necessary for enduring success.

Mechanisms for providing such tools include funding continuing education coursework, sponsoring college tuition reimbursement programs, and providing on-site educational seminars for personnel. Employees who receive such institutional assistance will have both the ability and the desire to return the investment through service excellence.

ACTING SMALL

Large and small nonprofit organizations each possess advantages and disadvantages associated with scale. Large nonprofit entities have the luxury of economies of scale, more notoriety, and a larger customer base. Smaller nonprofit entities, however, possess their share of advantages, too. These include nimbleness, less bureaucracy, and more personal service.

Given the ever-changing nature of the environment, coupled with increasing customer demands for personal service and attention, nonprofit entities would do well to remember the positive attributes associated with small entities and ensure that these characteristics are incorporated into their operations.

BRAND CULTIVATION

Through branding, nonprofit entities give their products identity. Brand identity greatly assists customers in the process of product differentiation and, therefore, represents a key source of competitive advantage.

Upstanding entities that successfully brand themselves and their products afford customers with assurances of quality that facilitate lasting patronage. Given the importance of branding, organizations must strive to cultivate and develop their brands in an effort to capitalize on the many associated benefits.

In some situations, particular nonprofit entities represent, in and of themselves, the brands to be cultivated. In other situations, units within nonprofit establishments may each represent brands to be cultivated. A large museum, for example, might seek to brand its multiple divisions (e.g., history, art, science, industry), as well as itself. Similarly, a college might brand its various schools, as well as itself, in an effort to capitalize on the benefits of branding.

GENEROSITY

Institutional generosity acts as a catalyst to all things good within organizations and even beyond. Acts of kindness (e.g., sponsoring student education programs, awarding scholarships to members of the community, supporting community initiatives) inspire customers, employees, suppliers, and communities. Generous acts firmly establish nonprofit organizations as true members of the greater community.

OPERATIONAL MATTERS

Clearly, nonprofit entities that incorporate the nine drivers of excellence identified by Berry are well on their way to achieving success in the marketplace. All too often, however, the tumultuous environment directs attention away from these important drivers of sustainable success, which is the reason many entities fail to meet and exceed the expectations of their target markets. Indeed, ensuring the presence of these drivers requires significant effort. Those nonprofit establishments that are willing to incorporate the success drivers into their daily operations position themselves for enduring growth and prosperity.

SUMMARY

Berry's Success Sustainability Model clearly illustrates the drivers of excellence that nonprofit entities must possess if they desire sustained growth and prosperity. Given the competitive nature of the marketplace, along with its environmental complexities, nonprofit organizations would do well to incorporate the nine drivers of excellence into their operations to reap the many benefits of sustained success.

EXERCISES

1. Provide a detailed overview of Leonard Berry's Success Sustainability Model, identifying and explaining its components, features, benefits, and value to nonprofit organizations. Add value to your discussion by including an illustration of this instrument, and be sure to preface your work by describing why excellence is an absolute necessity in the nonprofit sector.
2. Conduct a review of trade journals, websites, and other sources in an effort to identify articles profiling various nonprofit entities. From these profiles, seek to identify a specific nonprofit organization that appears to embrace the philosophy of Leonard Berry's Success Sustainability Model. Provide specific details as to how this organization measures up with the various components of the Success Sustainability Model. Be sure also to identify any areas where the entity appears to fall short or where information is insufficient to make a determination.

REFERENCE

Berry, L. L. (1999). *Discovering the soul of service: The nine drivers of sustainable business success*. New York, NY: The Free Press.

George Day's Market Orientation Model

INTRODUCTION

Progressive nonprofit executives understand that marketing success is largely based on how well they assess and address the markets they serve. This requires, among other things, the accurate assessment of customer wants and needs, the provision of products that effectively address those wants and needs, and the proactive assessment and management of competitive threats in the environment. Simply stated, these individuals understand the importance of being market driven.

When nonprofit executives adopt a market-driven mindset, they are perfectly positioned to capitalize on opportunities and avoid or eliminate threats in the environment. Through this proactive, externally focused stance, nonprofit executives are able to thoroughly understand their target markets and deliver product solutions that will earn confidence and trust, ultimately resulting in the enduring patronage of customers.

Despite the benefits associated with being market driven, many nonprofit executives fail to successfully incorporate this mindset, largely because of institutional systems that support inside-out, rather than outside-in, approaches. Entities embracing such inside-out approaches allow internal factors (e.g., prior histories and traditions, existing internal capabilities), rather than the externally based wants and needs of target markets, to guide operational decisions. Only by being market driven, an outside-in approach, can nonprofit organizations deliver superior customer value and reap the many benefits associated with this philosophy.

Nonprofit entities seeking to become market driven must shift their focus to the market. To provide guidance in achieving this transformation, George Day developed the Market Orientation Model, a diagram that presents the components of a market-driven organization. Illustrated in Figure 32-1, Day's Market Orientation Model consists

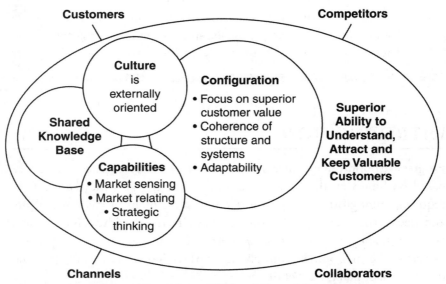

FIGURE 32-1 Day's Market Orientation Model

of an oval representing the internal environment of an organization, encompassing a series of four circles representing the entity's shared knowledge base and the three elements of a market orientation: culture, capabilities, and configuration. These three elements are defined as follows.

CULTURE

Culture, specifically one that is externally oriented, represents the first element of Day's Market Orientation Model. Culture can broadly be defined as the group of values, beliefs, and behaviors embraced by an organization. Every nonprofit organization possesses a culture that is unique to that particular entity. Depending on the composition of values, beliefs, and behaviors embraced, culture can positively or negatively influence operations and, when established, culture can be very difficult to change. Market-driven nonprofit organizations must possess an externally oriented, participative culture that heavily emphasizes the delivery of superior customer value and continually strives to secure new sources of competitive advantage.

A community college, for example, that seeks to establish an externally oriented culture must ensure that the appropriate constructs are in place to allow the culture to develop. One such construct is the institution's mission statement. As an openly circulated document, the mission statement is available for internal parties (e.g., administrators, faculty, staff), as well as external parties (e.g., stakeholders, students, suppliers), to view and quickly understand the community college's purpose.

When used appropriately, the mission statement serves as a guide for nonprofit executives and employees to follow in their many operational pursuits. It, therefore, is an excellent starting point for building an externally oriented culture. In order to do this, community college officials develop a mission statement that incorporates the elements of an externally oriented culture (i.e., an external, participative orientation emphasizing customer value and the continual search for competitive advantage) and take steps to ensure that they, along with other institutional members, base their actions on this statement. Such a mission statement greatly facilitates the establishment of an externally oriented culture.

CAPABILITIES

Capabilities represents the second element of Day's Market Orientation Model. Specifically, market-driven organizations must possess distinctive capabilities in the areas of *market sensing* (i.e., the ability to accurately assess and understand markets), *market relating* (i.e., the ability to create and maintain relationships with customers), and *strategic thinking* (i.e., the ability to devise successful strategies that proactively, rather than reactively, address marketplace opportunities and threats). With this set of capabilities, nonprofit executives are able to gain a thorough understanding of the customers and markets they serve. They also are able to strategically address associated environmental issues.

The necessity for having these capabilities is all the more essential in today's marketplace, which is characterized by innovation, intense competition, and uncertainty. Given this turbulent environment, nonprofit executives must ensure that they acquire and develop market-sensing, market-relating, and strategic-thinking capabilities, as they are ultimately the individuals looked to by others in their organizations to provide guidance in environmental assessment and strategic action.

CONFIGURATION

Configuration represents the third and final element of Day's Market Orientation Model. This element specifically involves the establishment of an organization-wide structure that allows all units within entities to proactively address changing customer requirements and marketplace conditions. In keeping with the attributes associated with market-driven nonprofit organizations, the particular configuration must emphasize the delivery of superior customer value, incorporate coherence between institutional structures and systems, and be adaptable to meet environmental challenges.

The configuration element of Day's Market Orientation Model essentially involves the creation of an institution-wide environment that fosters the development of a market orientation within every departmental unit. This orientation is particularly beneficial for large, complex nonprofit establishments that could never hope to be market driven without creating a configuration that fosters such a mindset across all organizational units.

OPERATIONAL MATTERS

It is important to understand that to be market driven, the three elements of culture, capabilities, and configuration must be supported by a shared knowledge base. Essentially, entities must ensure that information is openly shared interorganizationally in an effort to improve overall institutional performance.

All too often, information is poorly disseminated within nonprofit organizations. This shortfall is caused by a variety of factors, including poor communications systems, interorganizational conflict, and so on. Regardless of the reasons for poor information dissemination, nonprofit entities must take steps to open communications channels so that information can flow freely, providing the requisite shared knowledge base that supports the three elements of culture, capabilities, and configuration.

SUMMARY

Day's Market Orientation Model provides guidance in the assembly of work environments that are externally, rather than internally, focused. By incorporating this philosophy, nonprofit executives and their organizations become market driven and are perfectly positioned to capitalize on opportunities and avoid or eliminate threats in the environment, increasing the likelihood of successful endeavors.

EXERCISES

1. Define and comprehensively discuss George Day's Market Orientation Model, its components, and its value as an instrument for the assembly of market-driven mindsets in nonprofit institutions. A diagram of the Market Orientation Model should be included to add value to your narrative. Do you believe nonprofit institutions have become more or less market driven over the past several decades? Why do you believe this to be the case?
2. Place yourself in the role of top executive for a hypothetical, soon-to-be-launched nonprofit entity of your choice in your local community. Using George Day's Market Orientation Model,

craft a business plan that addresses each of the model's elements, ultimately in an effort to develop and sustain a market-driven mindset within the organization.

REFERENCE

Day, G. S. (1999). *The market driven organization: Understanding, attracting, and keeping valuable customers.* New York, NY: The Free Press.

33

Blake and Mouton's Sales Grid

INTRODUCTION

Personal selling is a promotional method involving the use of a sales force to convey messages. This promotional method is used extensively in the nonprofit sector; most notably in the many roles involving the solicitation of funds and other resources from donors, although the title "sales representative" is not typically used. Personal selling is also used in areas that are not traditionally associated with this promotional method. For example, the social workers and other outreach personnel of nursing homes who visit area hospitals, working to place those in need of skilled nursing services, are essentially serving as sales agents for their given facilities.

The specific job titles carried by those involved in personal selling in the nonprofit sector are highly varied, ranging from community liaison to outreach coordinator to donor recruiter and more. Regardless of the particular designation, this chapter will refer to all of those serving in such positions simply as sales representatives. They are hired to drive sales, whether that particular sales task involves increasing the number of blood donors, bolstering the box office receipts of a community theater, increasing the number of individuals committed to tobacco-free lifestyles, or encouraging the public to support a new sports stadium.

Sales representatives are often evaluated using some sort of quota, where performance is measured by comparing actual sales with preconceived sales goals for a given time period. This practice accurately assesses sales outcomes but does little to assess the techniques that sales representatives use to carry out their assigned duties and responsibilities. The sales approaches used by representatives are certainly of great importance to nonprofit entities. Sales agents do, after all, represent their employers. With the introduction of the Sales Grid, an evaluative tool developed by Robert Blake and Jane Mouton, the process of assessing the techniques used by sales representatives was greatly enhanced.

Illustrated in Figure 33-1, Blake and Mouton's Sales Grid consists of a nine-point horizontal scale that measures concern for the sale and a nine-point vertical scale that measures concern for the customer. On these scales, nine represents maximum concern and one represents minimum concern. A sales representative is evaluated first on his or her concern for the sale and then on his or her concern for the customer. This evaluation yields a two-number score that describes the sales representative's approach to selling. Of the 81 possible combinations on the Sales Grid, Blake and Mouton specifically identify and describe five, which are explained as follows.

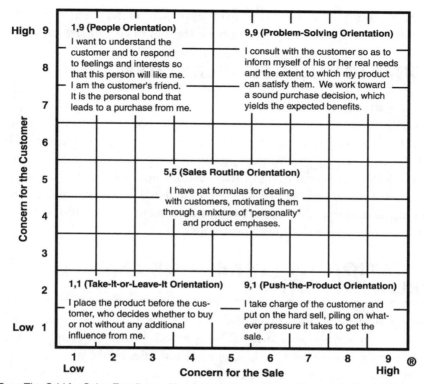

From The Grid for Sales Excellence: New Insights into a Proven System of Effective Sales, 2nd ed. by Robert R. Blake and Jane Srygley Mouton. Copyright © 1980, 1970 by Robert R. Blake and Jane Srygley Mouton. Published by McGraw-Hill. Sales Grid Copyright © Grid International, Inc. Reprinted by permission of Grid International, Inc.

FIGURE 33-1 Blake & Mouton's Sales Grid

LOCATION 9,1 (PUSH-THE-PRODUCT ORIENTATION)

The 9,1 strategy, located in the lower right corner of the Sales Grid, involves a complete concern for making the sale with little or no regard for the customer. Due to its total focus on making the sale, this strategy is termed the push-the-product orientation. Sales agents with such orientations use hard sell, pressure-oriented tactics to generate sales. Their concern for the sale is so pronounced that it is to the detriment of customers.

Quite obviously, customers resent this approach. Here, there is virtually no concern for the needs, preferences, or feelings of customers.

LOCATION 1,9 (PEOPLE ORIENTATION)

The 1,9 strategy, located in the upper left corner of the Sales Grid, involves little or no concern for the sale and maximum concern for the customer; hence the term *people orientation*. Sales representatives who practice this strategy seek to develop bonds with customers in hopes that sales will be generated through these relationships. Very little direct persuasion is used in their sales pitches. To the detriment of themselves and their organizations, salespersons become dependent on friendships, rather than effective sales techniques, for success.

LOCATION 1,1 (TAKE-IT-OR-LEAVE-IT ORIENTATION)

The 1,1 strategy, located in the Sales Grid's lower left corner, is termed the take-it-or-leave-it orientation. This approach involves little or no concern for both the sale and the customer. These sales representatives operate in a passive manner, doing nothing to develop customer relationships or communicate product features and benefits. Products are simply placed before customers who make purchase decisions without any assistance or influence from sales agents. With complete disregard for both sales and customers, these sales representatives serve to the detriment of all parties involved—themselves, their organizations, and their customers.

LOCATION 5,5 (SALES ROUTINE ORIENTATION)

The 5,5 strategy, located in the center of the Sales Grid, represents a middle-of-the-road approach. Termed the sales routine orientation, this approach involves a moderate amount of concern for both the sale and the customer. Here, sales representatives seek to make customers comfortable through light conversation and small talk as they present their pat formulas for generating sales. Their pat formulas are well-rehearsed sales presentations that come across rather mechanically. Although their performance is not stellar, sales representatives using this approach do achieve adequate results.

LOCATION 9,9 (PROBLEM-SOLVING ORIENTATION)

The 9,9 strategy, located in the Sales Grid's upper right corner, is termed the problem-solving orientation. This approach involves maximum concern for both the sale and the customer. Sales representatives using this strategy possess a highly detailed knowledge of both the products they sell and the specific needs of their customers. Here, sales agents work closely with customers to assist them in making sound decisions that meet and exceed expectations, yielding desired benefits.

These sales representatives provide solutions for customers. Given its maximum concern for both the sale and the customer, the 9,9 strategy yields superior results. Sales representatives who practice this strategy are assets to both their organizations and the customers they serve. Clearly, the 9,9 strategy is the most desirable sales approach.

OPERATIONAL MATTERS

Nonprofit executives can greatly benefit by using Blake and Mouton's Sales Grid to assess the techniques embraced by their sales representatives. By evaluating these techniques, they can identify strengths and weaknesses within their sales operations, taking corrective actions when necessary to ensure superior performance.

Figure 33-2 illustrates the usefulness of the Sales Grid. Here, a long term care system has evaluated each of its 12 sales representatives (i.e., community outreach liaisons) and plotted the resulting scores on the Sales Grid using an "X" accompanied by each sales agent's initials. This grid reveals that the system's sales force primarily uses sales techniques that are pitched toward the 9,9 problem-solving orientation. Notably, it also identifies a few sales agents whose techniques warrant alteration.

Not only is the Sales Grid useful as an assessment tool, but it is also useful as a training tool—particularly for new sales representatives. By instilling the 9,9 approach in sales trainees, these new recruits will be fully aware of the importance of carrying out their duties and responsibilities

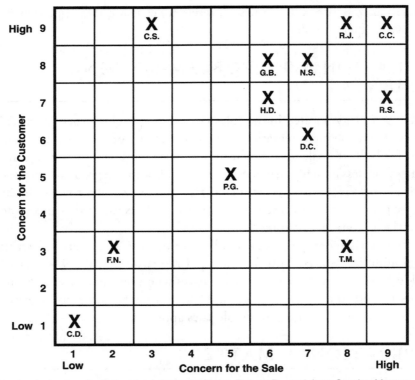

Constructed using design methodologies in Blake, Robert R., and Jane Srygley Mouton. 1980. The grid for sales excellence: New insights into a proven system of effective sales. 2nd ed. New York: McGraw-Hill.

FIGURE 33-2 A Sales Force Assessment Using the Sales Grid

in a problem-solving fashion. The Sales Grid can also be employed as a self-assessment tool for sales representatives. When used in this manner, sales representatives are reminded of desirable and undesirable approaches to selling and can alter their techniques accordingly.

Although the Sales Grid is primarily designed as a tool for the evaluation of sales representatives, it can also be used to assess any occupation that involves customer contact. Whenever employees come into contact with customers, they become sales representatives for their establishments and the Sales Grid applies. When viewed in this manner, the Sales Grid becomes a helpful tool for evaluating the customer service techniques of virtually any employee, from top executives down to entry-level personnel.

SUMMARY

Blake and Mouton's Sales Grid serves as an effective tool for evaluating the techniques used by sales representatives in carrying out their duties and responsibilities. It can also productively assess the approaches of all other employees who come into contact with customers. By using the Sales Grid, nonprofit executives can ensure that all employees charged with engaging customers are performing at optimal levels.

EXERCISES

1. Provide a detailed overview of Blake and Mouton's Sales Grid, discussing its design, structure, value, and use as an evaluative tool in the nonprofit sector. Be sure to include in your discussion insights as to how the Sales Grid can complement traditional sales outcomes assessments and serve as a training tool. Also provide insights into how the Sales Grid can be used to evaluate personnel who are serving in roles outside of formal sales positions.
2. Contact an area nonprofit entity that is engaged in personal selling of some sort. Arrange an interview with the organization's top executive to discuss sales force assessment approaches. During the interview, present the executive with Blake and Mouton's Sales Grid and request completion of the instrument. Looking at the aggregate results, how would you characterize the entity's sales force? Prepare a narrative of insights gained from your interview and associated findings.

REFERENCE

Blake, R. R., & Mouton, J. S. (1980). *The grid for sales excellence: New insights into a proven system of effective sales* (2nd ed.). New York, NY: McGraw-Hill.

Ries and Trout's Marketing Warfare Strategies

LEARNING OBJECTIVES

After examining this chapter, readers will have the ability to:

- Realize that competition represents one of the most significant obstacles to capturing and retaining market share.
- Recognize that nonprofit executives must not only be customer oriented but also competitor oriented to gain market share and achieve lasting success.
- Recognize the value offered by Ries and Trout's Marketing Warfare Strategies for assistance in understanding and implementing competitor-oriented marketing strategies that can be employed to increase market share.

INTRODUCTION

Nonprofit organizations must attract and retain customers to achieve growth and prosperity. Success at attracting and retaining customers ultimately determines the share of the market held by entities.

Market share is defined as an entity's portion, expressed as a percentage, of the total sales generated by a given product in a given market.

The entity that possesses the greatest market share is known as the market leader—an enviable position to hold.

One of the most significant obstacles to gaining market share is that of competition. The term *competition* brings to mind images of contests, challenges, and so on, and is a quite fitting descriptor for the marketplace. However, two authors view the marketing process as so intensely competitive that it deserves a more intense analogy—war.

In their book entitled *Marketing Warfare*, Al Ries and Jack Trout contend that "marketing is war" and apply warfare strategies and tactics to the marketing process. Ries and Trout specifically note that being customer oriented alone is not enough to achieve marketing success. Entities must also be competitor oriented, directing attention to the identification of competitors and the analysis of their strengths and weaknesses in an effort to wage marketing war.

To be successful, marketing campaigns must be planned like military campaigns. Nonprofit executives must, therefore, understand warfare principles and be able to implement these strategies and tactics effectively. For example, they must actively engage in the strategic planning process, seeking to formulate organizational goals and the action plans necessary for achieving these initiatives. They, too, must be skilled at anticipating competitive responses to various actions. Additionally, nonprofit executives must be proficient at gaining marketplace intelligence to plan and launch successful attacks. Importantly, they must also possess characteristics often associated with military leaders—character, perseverance, discipline, loyalty, and the like—to effectively wage marketing war.

According to Ries and Trout, marketing warfare can be waged using four different strategies: defensive warfare, offensive warfare, flanking warfare, and guerrilla warfare. As illustrated in Table 34-1, each strategy involves a number of basic, defining principles. The particular warfare strategy selected is dependent on the market position held by an entity. It should be noted that these strategies primarily apply to those nonprofit organizations that are engaged in market share pursuits in environments featuring competing entities, as opposed to those serving as providers of last resort where competition is of little or no concern. Using medical clinic examples, as these particular institutions often face intense competition in their given markets, these four marketing warfare strategies are explained as follows.

Table 34-1 Ries and Trout's Marketing Warfare Strategies

Defensive Warfare

Principle 1: Only the market leader should consider playing defense.

Principle 2: The best defensive strategy is the courage to attack yourself.

Principle 3: Strong competitive moves should always be blocked.

Offensive Warfare

Principle 1: The main consideration is the strength of the leader's position.

Principle 2: Find a weakness in the leader's strength and attack at that point.

Principle 3: Launch the attack on as narrow a front as possible.

Flanking Warfare

Principle 1: A good flanking move must be made into an uncontested area.

Principle 2: Tactical surprise ought to be an important element of the plan.

Principle 3: The pursuit is just as critical as the attack itself.

Guerrilla Warfare

Principle 1: Find a segment of the market small enough to defend.

Principle 2: No matter how successful you become, never act like the leader.

Principle 3: Be prepared to bug out at a moment's notice.

Source: Derived from information in Ries, A., & Trout, J. (1986). *Marketing warfare*. New York, NY: McGraw-Hill.

DEFENSIVE WARFARE

The defensive form of warfare should only be used by market leaders. Entities that possess such enviable positions should not, however, enter a hold-and-maintain mode. Instead, they should seek continuous improvement by attacking themselves. This improvement involves the routine introduction of new and enhanced offerings that render existing products obsolete. Such offerings ultimately improve the already positive market positions held by market leaders.

When rivals orchestrate strong competitive moves, market leaders must block these actions. One useful blocking technique involves copying the particular competitor's move. By copying a competitor's move, a tit-for-tat philosophy, entities can maintain their market leadership positions by leveraging their market dominance. Blocking ensures that market leadership does not erode.

The leading medical clinic in a community occupies the most powerful position in the minds of consumers. Obviously, the entity would like to maintain its leadership status. This goal, however, is not accomplished by complacency. Instead, the clinic must actively seek to attack itself by enhancing existing services and adding new services. The clinic might offer extended hours, a "no waiting" policy, or any other feature that improves its existing service array. If the clinic's market position is threatened by a rival, the establishment must vigorously counter the threat by copying the competitor's move. If, for example, a rival clinic seeks to increase its market share by opening a women's health division, the market leader should block the move by opening a similar unit. The leader's powerful market position gives it the upper hand even if it follows the move of a competitor.

OFFENSIVE WARFARE

Offensive warfare should be used by those entities falling just behind market leaders. These entities must target leaders, seeking to shift market share away from their powerful positions, preferably at points of weakness. Here, attacks should be initiated on very narrow fronts, perhaps on single products or small groups of offerings rather than entire product lines.

A clinic that finds itself trailing the market leader in a community has a much more difficult task at hand than that of the leader. The trailing clinic must, in essence, find ways to reduce the leader's market share, gathering the fallout to better its own market position. The clinic would do well to study the leader and select a front to charge. Perhaps the clinic could challenge the leader for its senior citizen patient base by emphasizing geriatric services. The leader, of course, could block the move, illustrating the difficult position of trailing entities in the battle for market share.

FLANKING WARFARE

The flanking warfare strategy is useful for any entity seeking to gain market share. This strategy involves the identification and occupation of new market segments. Although difficult to discover and develop, new segments offer open, uncontested terrain for flankers to occupy. The success of a flanking attack is largely related to the degree of surprise achieved. The element of surprise provides valuable time for flankers to establish beachheads within these new segments, making competitive responses much more difficult or even impossible. It is important to remember that after flanking attacks, nonprofit executives must diligently pursue the targeted market segments. All too often, entities fail to maintain the intensity of campaigns after initial marketing success. Attack and pursuit are of equally critical importance in the achievement of marketing success.

Newly discovered market segments offer growth opportunities for any clinic, regardless of its size or market position. The difficulty is in the discovery of these new segments. Increasing industrialization in a community might lead a clinic to address the increasing occupational health needs associated with this development. This new opportunity could be exploited for significant gains, resulting in control of the new segment. The more quickly the clinic targets and serves the new segment, the more likely its success as its rivals struggle to mount competitive responses. If success is achieved in the occupational health segment, the intensity demonstrated during the flanking attack must be maintained to ensure the entity's enduring dominance in the new segment.

GUERRILLA WARFARE

Guerrilla warfare is most appropriately used by smaller entities competing in a market of larger competitors. These smaller entities do not possess the resources to compete directly with market leaders. Instead, they must identify small market segments where they can maintain leadership positions. Small entities must understand and appreciate their status and never be lulled by success into behaving like market leaders. These small entities must be quick in every regard, entering segments when they become desirable and exiting segments when they become undesirable.

A small clinic in a community should select a target appropriate to its scale by pursuing a narrow segment within the larger market. The clinic might, for example, seek to be the preferred healthcare provider for individuals residing in a certain geographic area of the community. Importantly, this small clinic should respect its position in the broad market.

Regardless of its success, the clinic must avoid acting like the market leader. It must emphasize rapidity, which will enable it to capitalize on emerging opportunities.

SUMMARY

With their contention that "marketing is war," Ries and Trout provide a very useful, militaristic analogy for the marketing process. Their work is quite beneficial in that it introduces and advocates a competitor orientation to marketing and provides an array of strategies that can be employed to increase market share.

Given the competitive and complex nature of the marketplace, along with the necessity for entities to attract and retain customers, nonprofit executives would do well to remember the useful guidelines offered by Ries and Trout. The authors have accurately identified successful strategies for waging marketing war.

EXERCISES

1. Provide a detailed overview of Ries and Trout's Marketing Warfare Strategies, identifying and explaining each of the identified strategies, their criteria for use, and associated implications for the nonprofit sector. What are your thoughts on the accuracy and viability of the war analogy that Ries and Trout use to describe marketing?
2. Conduct a review of trade journals, websites, and other sources in an effort to identify articles profiling various nonprofit entities. For each of the four Marketing Warfare Strategies, find at least one nonprofit entity using the strategy. If your research reveals entities that appear to be going against the strategy advice provided by Ries and Trout, feel free to identify these, as well. Describe your findings in detail.

REFERENCE

Ries, A., & Trout, J. (1986). *Marketing warfare*. New York, NY: McGraw-Hill.

35

Philip Kotler's Marketing Plan

LEARNING OBJECTIVES

After examining this chapter, readers will have the ability to:

- Understand that nonprofit executives must formalize their marketing pursuits on at least an annual basis via the development of comprehensive marketing plans.
- Realize the value of marketing plans as instruments that compel nonprofit executives to think about upcoming periods, perform routine marketing analyses, and set marketing goals and objectives.
- Recognize that Philip Kotler's Marketing Plan provides a useful framework for developing these important devices.

INTRODUCTION

Given the scope and diversity of marketing activities, it is essential for nonprofit executives to formalize their pursuits on at least an annual basis through the development of comprehensive marketing plans. By putting marketing pursuits in writing, they are forced to think through upcoming periods, perform routine marketing analyses, and set marketing goals and objectives that are properly aligned with institutional goals and objectives.

When completed, marketing plans act as road maps, allowing nonprofit executives to assess their progress over time, making adjustments as necessary. Without formal marketing plans, nonprofit executives will likely find themselves managing marketing pursuits in a reactive fashion, lacking insight, direction, and control—a formula for disaster.

Developing marketing plans requires significant effort and attention. Among other things, these plans require accurate product, market, and competitor information, as well as insightful and creative thinking on the part of plan authors and contributors. Marketing plans also must be well written and presented in an orderly fashion—aspects that greatly enhance the usefulness of these documents.

Although there are no mandatory guidelines for the format of marketing plans, a quite useful outline for such plans has been offered by Philip Kotler. Illustrated in Table 35-1, Kotler's Marketing Plan consists of eight sections: an executive summary and table of contents, an overview of the current marketing situation, an opportunity and issue analysis, the identification of marketing objectives, the identification of the marketing strategies to be employed, the stipulation of action programs for attaining strategic objectives, the presentation of financial projections, and the identification of implementation controls for monitoring plan performance.

Table 35-1 Components of Kotler's Marketing Plan

Section 1: Executive summary and table of contents

Section 2: Current marketing situation

Section 3: Opportunity and issue analysis

Section 4: Objectives

Section 5: Marketing strategy

Section 6: Action programs

Section 7: Financial projections

Section 8: Implementation controls

Source: Derived from information in Kotler, P. (2003). *Marketing management* (11th ed.). Upper Saddle River, NJ: Prentice Hall.

SECTION 1: EXECUTIVE SUMMARY AND TABLE OF CONTENTS

Kotler's Marketing Plan begins with an executive summary and table of contents. The executive summary specifically provides a concise overview of plan contents, emphasizing main goals and recommendations. This summary allows readers to quickly review the major facets of associated marketing plans. The executive summary is followed by a table of contents, which outlines given marketing plans and provides a page numbering system to assist readers in locating major plan components. Although this section is listed first, it is by necessity, of course, developed last.

SECTION 2: CURRENT MARKETING SITUATION

The executive summary and table of contents section is followed by a review of the current marketing situation. Here, an overview of current marketing pursuits is presented, providing background information as necessary. This section includes information and analyses regarding customers, markets, and competitors, along with relevant performance data (e.g., sales, cost, and related information), providing readers with a comprehensive snapshot of current marketing efforts.

SECTION 3: OPPORTUNITY AND ISSUE ANALYSIS

After identifying the current marketing situation, an opportunity and issue analysis is presented. In this section, the strengths, weaknesses, opportunities, and threats associated with product offerings are identified. Methods for capitalizing on the identified strengths and opportunities are noted, as are methods for avoiding or eliminating weaknesses and threats.

After this information has been presented and addressed, relevant issues and concerns are identified. Such issues and concerns might include whether particular markets should be pursued; whether promotional expenditures should be increased or decreased; whether given products should continue to be offered, be discontinued, or be modified; and so on.

SECTION 4: OBJECTIVES

When opportunities and issues have been identified and addressed, broad marketing objectives for the upcoming period are presented. A blood bank, for example, might seek to increase its donor volume by 10% over the next six months. An antitobacco foundation might seek to reduce teen smoking by 20% over the next two years. A trade association might wish to increase memberships by 15% over the next year. Depending on the particular organization, the number of identified objectives might be as few as one or quite numerous.

SECTION 5: MARKETING STRATEGY

The objectives section of Kotler's Marketing Plan is followed by the identification of broad marketing strategies that will be used to achieve identified objectives. This section essentially presents the broad marketing game plan. The blood bank seeking to increase donor volume might designate a strategy of increasing public awareness of the lifesaving potential of such donations. The antitobacco foundation seeking to reduce teen smoking might devise a strategy involving the increased dissemination of its message in schools. The trade association seeking to increase memberships might formulate a strategy that involves improving membership benefits and increasing industry awareness of those benefits. These broad strategies are operationalized through the implementation of action programs identified in the following section.

SECTION 6: ACTION PROGRAMS

The marketing strategy section of Kotler's Marketing Plan is followed by the identification of action programs that specify how organizations plan to accomplish their broad marketing goals. The blood bank would list how it plans to increase consumer awareness, possibly through the development of a new advertising campaign. It would also identify the nature of the campaign, the advertising media to be used, the scheduling pattern for associated advertisements, and related data. The antitobacco foundation would identify the particular schools targeted by its campaign, the nature of the educational programs to be conveyed to students, the individuals responsible for conveyance of these programs, and the associated program delivery schedule. The trade association would discuss its specific plans for increasing memberships, providing detailed information related to membership upgrades and a possible new advertising campaign. Action programs are very specific and itemize the tactical operations necessary to carry out identified marketing strategies.

SECTION 7: FINANCIAL PROJECTIONS

After action programs have been identified, financial projections are presented, which stipulate expected financial outcomes and accompanying budgets. The revenue side of associated budgets presents anticipated cash inflows resulting from marketing efforts, while the expense side lists associated marketing costs (e.g., costs associated with advertising and distribution). The difference between the revenue side and the expense side of associated budgets serves as an indicator of plan viability.

SECTION 8: IMPLEMENTATION CONTROLS

The final section of Kotler's Marketing Plan identifies mechanisms for monitoring the progress of marketing pursuits. Importantly, this section includes a time line for implementing stipulated marketing activities and for reviewing associated results. Marketing progress should be formally monitored on either a monthly or a quarterly basis. This section also includes contingency plans for use in the event that undesirable results occur.

SUMMARY

The complex and varied array of marketing activities within organizations necessitates the development and assembly of formal marketing plans. These plans force nonprofit executives to think through upcoming periods, perform routine marketing analyses, and set appropriate marketing goals and objectives. When completed, marketing plans serve as road maps that guide nonprofit executives, allowing them to proactively, rather than reactively, address and manage marketing pursuits.

Given the importance of marketing plans, great care must be taken in preparing these documents. Kotler's Marketing Plan provides a useful framework for presenting these documents in an orderly fashion. By using Kotler's framework, nonprofit executives are assured that their marketing plans contain necessary plan components and that these elements are presented appropriately. When content is added to this framework, an invaluable marketing resource emerges.

EXERCISES

1. Provide a detailed account profiling Philip Kotler's Marketing Plan, identifying and explaining each of its eight steps. Share your thoughts on the degree to which modern nonprofit organizations adequately plan marketing pursuits via the development of formal marketing plans.

2. Contact a local nonprofit entity and arrange an informational interview with its top executive to gain insights into the organization's marketing planning process. Specifically, request information regarding the frequency of plan development, chief participants in plan design, methods for formulating goals and objectives, mechanisms for monitoring progress, and procedures for handling unforeseen circumstances that hamper original marketing plan designs. Report your findings in detail.

REFERENCE

Kotler, P. (2003). *Marketing management* (11th ed.). Upper Saddle River, NJ: Prentice Hall.

Appendix

An Introduction to Marketing

INTRODUCTION

Modern organizations compete in today's extremely competitive marketplace, in an environment of immense and ever-increasing complexity. On an ongoing basis, establishments of all kinds vie against one another in their respective markets for the opportunity to serve customers. Each of these organizations ultimately is in search of growth and prosperity, and the best managed of these entities will indeed realize this goal.

Marketing is possibly the most critical management responsibility associated with the pursuit and realization of growth and prosperity. Marketing can broadly be defined as a management process that involves the assessment of customer wants and needs, and the performance of all activities associated with the development, pricing, provision, and promotion of product solutions that satisfy those wants and needs. Although most often associated with advertising and sales, marketing is much more encompassing, as this definition implies. Aside from promotions activities, marketing includes such critical functions as environmental scanning, wants and needs assessment, new product development, target marketing, product pricing, product distribution, and market research.

WANTS AND NEEDS

Marketing pursuits normally begin with assessing the wants and needs of customers. The terms *want* and *need* are often used interchangeably in society; however, these words are actually quite distinct, particularly when associated with marketing goods and services. A *need* is something that a person requires for well-being and possibly survival, while a *want* is something that a person simply desires.

Items such as food, water, electricity for the home, and gasoline for automobile transportation to work are purchased and consumed out of necessity and, therefore, represent needs. Vacation getaways, jewelry, civic club memberships, and trips to the local museum or zoo, however, represent wants in that the products are not necessities.

PRODUCTS: GOODS AND SERVICES

The marketplace is filled with countless wants and needs, with rewards being offered to organizations that can satisfy those wants and needs with product solutions. The term *product* refers to any offering provided by an entity for purchase and consumption. A product can be a good (i.e., a tangible item), a service (i.e., an intangible item), or a hybrid (i.e., an item with tangible and intangible characteristics). This array of product variants can be illustrated on a continuum with tangible items at one end and intangible items at the other end. Figure A-1 illustrates this continuum along with several example products that have been placed on the continuum based on their tangibility or lack thereof.

Pure goods, such as jewelry, furniture, and sports equipment, can be viewed in reasonable isolation from any service component, while pure services, including haircuts, education, physical examinations, and public transportation, can be isolated from any tangible offering.

Food ordered at a restaurant, however, represents a hybrid product in that a service (waitstaff assistance and food preparation) must accompany the good that is provided (the particular meal that was ordered).

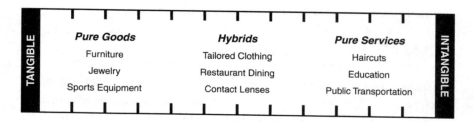

FIGURE A-1 The Product Continuum

Prescription contact lenses would also represent a hybrid product in that a service (diagnosis by a medical professional) must accompany the delivery of the good that is provided (the particular contact lenses).

Beyond goods and services, it is important to note that ideas and philosophies can also be considered products—intangible, of course. Political candidates campaigning for public office and cause-related organizations seeking to encourage particular actions (e.g., charitable donations, healthy lifestyles), are, in essence, attempting to sell products to designated populations.

Regardless of their tangibility or lack thereof, products that ineffectively address the wants and needs of customers will surely fail. By appropriately addressing customer wants and needs, the likelihood that associated goods and services will achieve commercial success is increased.

TARGET MARKETING

When new products are developed, organizations must determine which customer groups they wish to pursue and how they wish to present their products to these groups—a practice known as target marketing. Through target marketing, product offerings and associated marketing activities are customized in an effort to address the wants and needs of specific customer groups.

Target marketing involves three interrelated activities: market segmentation, targeting, and product positioning. Market segmentation is the process of dividing a market into groups (i.e., segments) of individuals who share common characteristics. Once the market has been segmented, targeting ensues where attractive segments are selected (i.e., targeted), permitting focused efforts on satisfying the wants and needs of these groups. These targeted segments are known as an entity's target market. Product positioning follows targeting and involves the determination of an appropriate and effective image to convey to customers. Positioning efforts seek to influence customer perceptions related to particular goods and services.

Usefully, target marketing permits the development of customized promotional campaigns designed to appeal to given segments. This customization increases the likelihood that target markets will respond favorably to product offerings. Target marketing also permits promotions resources to be utilized more efficiently because marketing efforts can be directed toward specific audiences rather than entire markets.

THE MARKETING MIX

Upon identification of the particular segment or segments to pursue, attention is directed toward formulating the marketing mix for each customer group that is sought. Illustrated in Figure A-2, the marketing mix includes four interdependent components: product, price, place, and promotion. It is often referred to as the four Ps of marketing. For each product offering, each component of the marketing mix must be formulated in a manner that will entice target markets.

Product

The product component of the marketing mix involves the development of goods and services that will meet and, ideally, exceed the wants and needs of target markets. For goods, product development involves, among other things, the actual physical assembly of the offerings. For services, product development involves the assembly of all components required

FIGURE A-2 The Marketing Mix

for the services to be offered, such as office space, equipment, operating permits, and personnel.

Great care must be taken in assembling product attributes for targeted customer segments. An appropriate fit between given product offerings and the wants and needs of target audiences is an essential requirement for marketing success.

Price

The price component of the marketing mix involves all elements associated with pricing products in a manner that will be attractive to target markets. Price is defined as the amount of money that must be paid by customers in order to acquire particular goods and services.

The more features embedded into products, the greater they cost organizations to produce and provide. These costs, of course, are ultimately passed on to customers, directly or indirectly, in the form of higher prices. Plush office spaces located in the community's highest traffic areas, the latest technologies, elaborate and extensive product arrays, exceptional customer service, and so on, all add to the costs associated with providing goods and services.

There are, of course, limits to what individuals (or where applicable, third-party payers) can and will pay for goods and services. Broadly speaking, a balance must be struck between the attributes of particular products and the prices charged for the offerings. This balance must meet the financial requirements of organizations and the financial means of prospective customers—items that must be thoroughly addressed prior to bringing products to market.

Place

The place component of the marketing mix, which is sometimes termed *distribution*, refers to all elements involved in making products available to customers. These activities include such tasks as the identification of distribution channels, the determination of inventory levels, and the management of warehousing issues. Other place activities include determining locations of availability and hours of operation.

Different products often require different place considerations. Public transportation providers would be concerned with fleet acquisition and maintenance, as well as the determination of appropriate and desirable transit routes and schedules. Food banks would be concerned with establishing an array of distribution linkages ultimately resulting in their food items reaching the needy. Medical clinics would be concerned with such place matters as the physical location and hours of operation of their establishments. Meal delivery charities would focus heavily on their geographic service areas and delivery time lines. Colleges and universities would direct attention toward determining when and where courses are offered to students.

Consumption cannot occur if product offerings are not accessible to target markets, with ease of access positively influencing consumption. The place component of the marketing mix focuses on hastening the purchase process by making goods and services readily available to customers.

Promotion

The promotion component of the marketing mix involves all activities associated with communicating product attributes to target markets. Advertising is perhaps the best-known promotional method; however, other forms exist, including personal selling, sales promotion, public relations, and direct marketing. These five promotional methods combine to form what is referred to as the promotions, or communications, mix.

Organizations normally promote themselves using a variety of methods in their quest to entice customers to purchase and consume products. These communicative techniques build product awareness by engaging potential customers and encouraging their patronage through the conveyance of product attributes—the domain of the promotion component of the marketing mix.

ONGOING MARKETING SURVEILLANCE

Throughout the marketing process, a keen awareness of the environment must be maintained by engaging in ongoing marketing surveillance. Marketing surveillance activities include assessing customer wants and needs, assessing the potential of markets, identifying market trends, monitoring product performance in given markets, monitoring the activities of competitors, and determining future marketing pursuits. Importantly, surveillance activities must be sustained over time—an absolute necessity given the ever-changing nature of the marketplace.

SUMMARY

Marketing is possibly the most critical management responsibility associated with the pursuit and realization of growth and prosperity. Organizations must ensure that they devote sufficient resources to marketing and its many activities. Institutional success is directly linked to success in marketing.

Glossary

Adoption Process   A series of progressive steps leading up to the purchase and consumption of new products.

Advertisement   A verbal and/or visual message that is designed to inform potential customers of product offerings and attract their patronage, forwarded via mass media.

Advertising   A promotional method involving the paid use of mass media to deliver messages. Examples include newspaper, magazine, radio, television, and billboard advertisements.

Advertising Agency   An organization that exists for the purpose of developing and placing advertisements, and typically other forms of promotion, on behalf of paying clients.

Advocacy Advertising   Advertising that promotes a political, economic, social, or technological perspective of an entity, often calling for audiences to modify their behavior to adhere to given points of view.

All-You-Can-Afford Budgeting Method   An advertising budgeting method where operational expenditures are identified and funded across given organizations, with the remaining resources (i.e., that which is left-over after all other expenses have been paid) being assigned to fund advertising initiatives in the forthcoming period.

Antitrust Laws   Laws designed and developed to promote competition by forbidding monopolies.

Atmosphere   The aesthetic qualities of the environment of a particular establishment, which combine to form an ambiance that has the ability to positively or negatively influence customers.

Audience   (1) The population that has been selected (i.e., targeted) by an organization for pursuit as customers. Also referred to as a target audience, target market, or target population. (2) The population that is exposed to a given mass-media vehicle and is thus exposed to associated promotional messages.

Audience Fragmentation   A term used to characterize the dispersion of broad audiences resulting from the proliferation of various media sources that divide audiences into increasingly smaller groups, making it more difficult for marketers to conveniently reach target populations.

Availabilities   Units of advertising (e.g., space in outdoor advertising, airtime in television advertising) that are available for purchase on a given date. In practice, the term is more commonly used in its abbreviated form: *avails.*

Bait-and-Switch Advertising   A form of deceptive advertising involving the promotion of a particular product, often at a very attractive price, as a means of generating customer traffic. When interested customers inquire about the advertised product, they are instead offered another item— typically carrying a higher price than the advertised offering—under the guise that the advertised product is of poor quality, has sold out, or is otherwise unavailable or inappropriate for their needs.

Barriers to Entry   Anything that blocks or otherwise prohibits an entity from entering and competing in a given market (e.g., regulations, capital requirements, superior competition).

Benchmarking   The practice of comparing the marketing performance of an organization and/or its product offerings to established standards of excellence known as benchmarks.

Billboard   A stationary advertising structure that is placed along transit pathways to display promotional messages to passersby.

Billboard Advertising   A form of outdoor advertising involving the use of stationary structures that are placed along transit pathways to display promotional messages to passersby. Standard billboard advertising products include the 8-sheet poster (6'×12'), the 30-sheet poster (12'3"×24'6"), and the bulletin (10'6"×36', 14'×48', and other sizes).

Black Market   An illegal market that develops when goods and services are exchanged in violation of governmental restrictions prohibiting such transactions.

Brainstorming   An activity involving intensive discussion and thought regarding a particular matter of concern for the purpose of generating applicable ideas, solutions, and so on.

Brand   A name, logo, slogan, or other reference that identifies goods and services, thus allowing consumers to differentiate product offerings.

Brand Equity   The value of a brand.

Brand Extension   The application of an established product's brand name to a new product in an effort to capitalize on existing brand awareness.

Brand Loyalty   An intense commitment to a particular brand resulting from a customer's prior positive experiences with the given brand.

Brand Portfolio   The overall collection of brands held by an organization.

Branding   The process of developing, assigning, and managing names, logos, slogans, and other identifiers associated with products.

Buyer   (1) An individual who purchases a product either for his or her own use or on behalf of another party. (2) An individual who, as part of his or her formal employment duties, purchases designated products on behalf of an organization for use in accomplishing a given mission.

Call to Action   A request, forwarded by an advertisement, calling on audience members to respond in some desired manner (e.g., to purchase a product).

Cannibalism   The introduction of a product that either partially or completely serves as a substitute for an existing product held by the same organization, thus diminishing the sales associated with the existing item.

Caveat Emptor   A Latin phrase meaning "let the buyer beware," which serves to remind consumers of the need to investigate given products and the entities that provide them prior to completing a purchase in the marketplace.

Channel of Distribution   A pathway through which products are routed from their producers to the end users of associated offerings. This pathway can be direct, with products flowing directly from producer to consumer, or indirect, with products flowing from producer to consumer through one or more intermediaries (e.g., wholesalers, retailers).

Clutter   A term used to describe elements in the environment (e.g., competing advertising messages, distractions) that compete with the marketing communications of given establishments for the attention of target audiences. Also termed *noise*.

Co-branding   The practice of applying two brand names, each held by different organizations, to a given product offering in an effort to capitalize on the synergies afforded by combined brand identity.

Commercialization   The full-scale marketplace introduction of newly developed product offerings.

Communications Mix   The five promotional methods used by marketers to reach target audiences: advertising, personal selling, sales promotion, public relations, and direct marketing. Also referred to as the *promotions mix*.

Comparative Advertisement   An advertisement that presents the features and benefits of a product in relation to competitive offerings in an effort to demonstrate product superiority for the purpose of encouraging exchange.

Competitive Advantage   Anything possessed by an organization that gives it an edge over its competitors.

Competitive Parity Budgeting Method   An advertising budgeting method where marketers estimate the level of funding that their competitors direct toward advertising and then fund their advertising budgets accordingly, essentially matching the advertising resources of their competitors.

Concept Testing   The practice of seeking consumer feedback regarding a hypothetical product offering or advertising message to gauge related interest and enthusiasm.

Continuity   An advertising scheduling strategy that involves the even, consistent delivery of advertising messages over an extended period of time.

Cooperative Advertising An advertising arrangement where two entities, often the retailer of a product and its manufacturer, agree to share the costs of given advertisements, yielding reduced per-entity advertising expenditures and increased sales that will be enjoyed by both parties.

Cost The amount of money that entities must spend to produce and/or provide goods and services.

Cost per Thousand (CPM) A term, abbreviated CPM, which reflects the advertising costs necessary for a given advertising vehicle to reach an audience of 1,000 individuals. The "M" in CPM represents the Roman numeral for 1,000.

Customer Any party (e.g., an individual consumer, an institution) that purchases the goods and services of a given entity. The party may or may not be the end user of the purchased items.

Customer Relationship Management (CRM) A marketing practice involving the delivery of personalized attention, service, and support to target audiences in an effort to establish lasting bonds with customers, ensuring their enduring patronage.

Customer Satisfaction A primary goal of any business entity resulting from successful efforts to meet and, ideally, exceed the wants and needs of customers.

Demarketing A practice where marketers, notably in situations of scarcity, seek to lessen the demand for given product offerings by reducing or eliminating advertisements, discounts, and other purchase incentives.

Diffusion A term used to describe the gradual acceptance of a new product in the marketplace that occurs over time.

Direct Marketing A promotional method involving the delivery of messages directly to consumers. Examples include direct-mail marketing, telemarketing, and catalog marketing.

Distribution All elements involved with making products available to target markets. Examples include the transportation of goods to retail establishments, the warehousing of finished products, and the determination of hours of operation. Sometimes used as an alternative term for the *place* aspect of the marketing mix.

Electronic Advertising   Advertising that uses electronic media, notably including radio, television, and the Internet, to deliver promotional messages to target audiences.

Environmental Scanning   An externally focused activity where marketers seek to assess the environment in an effort to identify marketplace trends.

Exchange   A goal of marketing that involves the successful completion of a transaction between a buyer and a seller.

Flighting   An advertising scheduling strategy that involves the intermittent delivery of advertising messages to target audiences. It is characterized by intensive bursts of advertising, which are preceded and followed by periods of hiatus.

Four Ps of Marketing   The four interdependent components of product, price, place, and promotion that must be formulated for each product offering in an effort to attract target markets. Also known as the *marketing mix*.

Frequency   A measure of advertising effectiveness that specifically refers to the total number of times that individuals are exposed to a particular advertisement. Frequency (i.e., the number of exposures per individual) and reach (i.e., the number of individuals exposed) largely determine advertising impact (i.e., the degree to which given advertisements are effective).

Good   A tangible product offering.

Identity Management   A marketing practice involving the comprehensive management of all elements related to the establishment and maintenance of institutional and/or product identity, notably including branding and advertising.

Impact   A measure of the overall effectiveness of a given advertisement, which is largely determined by the reach (i.e., the number of individuals exposed) and frequency (i.e., the number of exposures per individual) achieved by the particular advertisement.

Integrated Marketing Communications   The coordination of all of the marketing communications efforts of an organization for the purpose of ensuring the consistent presentation of promotional messages to target audiences.

Intermediary   A participant in the process of routing goods and services from producers to the end users of associated product offerings. Also referred to as *channel members*, intermediaries include entities such as wholesalers and retailers.

Key Account   A customer who is responsible for a substantial portion of the total sales of a given entity and thus warrants special attention from the associated organization.

Line Extension   The addition of a new, and typically related, product offering to an existing array of products offered by an organization.

Macroenvironment   External forces within the marketplace that, although beyond the control of executives, have the potential to influence organizations. Such forces are often divided into four categories: political, economic, social, and technological.

Magazine Advertising   A form of print advertising that involves the use of magazines, typically circulated on a regular basis, to deliver promotional messages to target audiences.

Margin   The difference between the cost of producing and/or providing a product and the price received for the given offering.

Market   A broad collection of potential customers.

Market Leader   The entity or product, depending on the focus of the assessment, that possesses the greatest share of a given market.

Market Penetration   The degree to which a given product has acquired market share in a given market.

Market Potential   The overall capability of a given market to deliver customers for a given product, with such potential ranging from positive to negative from the perspective of marketers who are responsible for promoting the designated product.

Market Segment   A group of individuals within a market who share common characteristics (e.g., age, income, tastes, preferences).

Market Segmentation   The process of dividing a market into groups (i.e., segments) of individuals who share common characteristics. Market segmentation is the first step of target marketing.

Market Share   An entity's portion, expressed as a percentage, of the total sales generated by a given product in a given market.

Marketing   A management process that involves the assessment of customer wants and needs, and the performance of all activities associated with the development, pricing, provision, and promotion of product solutions that satisfy those wants and needs.

Marketing Concept   A marketing philosophy that became prevalent in the 1960s and remains so today, which recognizes and appreciates the valuable role of customers in marketing, leading marketers to focus their attention on meeting and exceeding the wants and needs of their target audiences.

Marketing Mix   The four interdependent components of product, price, place, and promotion that must be formulated for each product offering in an effort to attract target markets. Also known as the four Ps of marketing.

Marketing Plan   A formal document that describes and assesses the current marketing performance of an organization and sets marketing goals and objectives for the upcoming period.

Mass Marketing   The practice of offering products to the market as a whole without regard for the individual tastes and preferences of consumers.

Mass Media   A term that refers to the range of media vehicles (e.g., newspapers, magazines, radio, television, billboards) that can be used to deliver promotional messages to large target audiences.

Microenvironment   Internal forces within an organization that have the potential to influence the given establishment. Such forces include capital, personnel, institutional capabilities, and so on.

Need   Something that is required for well-being and possibly survival. A necessity as opposed to a desire.

New Product Development   The creation of a new good or service usually resulting from a systematic process ranging from idea conception to commercialization.

New-to-the-World Product   A newly introduced product that defines an entirely new product category never before offered to the public.

Newspaper Advertising   A form of print advertising that involves the use of newspapers, typically circulated on a daily or weekly basis, to deliver promotional messages to target audiences.

Niche Marketing   A practice where marketers target and intensively focus on fulfilling the wants and needs of a very defined segment of the market in an effort to serve that particular segment better than any other entity in the marketplace.

Noise   A term used to describe elements in the environment (e.g., competing advertising messages, distractions) that compete with the marketing communications of given establishments for the attention of target audiences. Also termed *clutter*.

Objective-and-Task Budgeting Method   An advertising budgeting method that involves the independent, ground-up development of an advertising budget based on the promotional wants and needs of an institution. Advertising objectives are identified, along with the tasks required to accomplish those objectives, and a budget is formulated accordingly.

Outdoor Advertising   Advertising that uses billboards, transit vehicles, street furniture, and other out-of-home media to deliver promotional messages to target audiences.

Outshopping   A practice where consumers in a given marketplace forgo the goods and services offered by organizations in their particular community, choosing instead to purchase the products from other vendors in adjacent marketplaces.

Packaging   The exterior boxes, cartons, wrappers, and similar elements that are used to aid in the transportation of products to given sales locations and in the presentation of offerings to potential buyers.

Percentage-of-Sales Budgeting Method   An advertising budgeting method that calls for marketers to review sales for the previous period and determine an appropriate percentage that should be dedicated to advertising. The resulting amount then serves as the advertising budget for the forthcoming period.

Personal Selling   A promotional method involving the use of a sales force to convey messages to target audiences.

Place   One of the four Ps of marketing, involving the formulation of all elements associated with making products available to target markets. Examples include the transportation of goods to retail establishments, the warehousing of finished products, and the determination of hours of operation. Sometimes referred to as *distribution*.

Portfolio Analysis   An activity involving the comprehensive review and assessment of an organization's product offerings.

Price   (1) The amount of money that must be paid by customers to acquire particular goods and services. (2) One of the four Ps of marketing, involving all elements associated with pricing products in a manner that will be attractive to target markets.

Print Advertising   Advertising that uses print media, notably including newspapers and magazines, to deliver promotional messages to target audiences.

Product   (1) Any offering provided by an entity for purchase and consumption. A product can be a good (i.e., a tangible item), a service (i.e., an intangible item), or a hybrid (i.e., an item with tangible and intangible characteristics). (2) One of the four Ps of marketing, involving the development of goods and services that will meet and, ideally, exceed the wants and needs of target markets.

Product Class   A collection of similar to diverse product offerings that serve related wants and needs.

Product Deletion   The elimination of a particular good or service from a given product portfolio.

Product Differentiation   (1) The ability to distinguish goods and services from competitive offerings. (2) The development of distinguishable product features that allow offerings to easily be recognized by customers.

Product Form   A particular manifestation of a product and its closely related variants.

Product Life Cycle   A model that illustrates the four stages of a product's development: introduction, growth, maturity, and decline.

Product Portfolio   The overall collection of products held by an organization.

Product Positioning   The process of determining an appropriate and effective image for products to convey to customers in an effort to influence their perceptions of goods and services. Product positioning is the final step of target marketing.

Production Concept   A marketing philosophy, prevalent during the 1800s and early 1900s, that emphasized the production of goods and services, leading marketers to focus their attention on excellence in this area, typically at the expense of customers and their defined wants and needs.

Promotion   (1) All activities associated with communicating a product's attributes to target markets. (2) One of the four Ps of marketing, involving the formulation of communications strategies and tactics that will effectively convey product attributes to target markets.

Promotions Mix   The five promotional methods used by marketers to reach target audiences: advertising, personal selling, sales promotion, public relations, and direct marketing. Also referred to as the *communications mix*.

Public Relations   A promotional method involving the use of publicity and other unpaid forms of promotion to deliver messages. Examples include press releases, open houses, facility tours, and educational seminars.

Pull Strategy   A marketing communications strategy that involves directing communicative efforts (e.g., advertising, sales promotion, direct marketing) toward consumers who, in turn, demand the associated products from establishments in the marketplace. Such activities essentially pull given products through channels of distribution, resulting in exchange.

Pulsing   An advertising scheduling strategy that involves the placement of a consistent but tempered number of advertising messages over a given campaign period, supplemented periodically by surges in the quantity of messages delivered to target audiences.

Push-Pull Strategy   A marketing communications strategy that involves directing communicative efforts (e.g., advertising, sales promotion, direct marketing) toward both intermediaries and consumers in the marketplace in an attempt to generate exchange.

Push Strategy   A marketing communications strategy that involves directing communicative efforts (e.g., advertising, personal selling, sales promotion, direct marketing) toward intermediaries who purchase the associated offerings and, in turn, promote them to their customers. Such activities essentially push given products through channels of distribution, resulting in exchange.

Radio Advertising   A form of electronic advertising that uses radio to deliver promotional messages to target audiences.

Rate Card   A document prepared by a media firm (e.g., a radio or television station, a newspaper or magazine publisher, an outdoor advertising plant operator) that lists various rates for given advertising purchases.

Reach   A measure of advertising effectiveness that specifically refers to the total number of individuals who are exposed to a particular advertisement. Reach (i.e., the number of individuals exposed) and frequency (i.e., the number of exposures per individual) largely determine advertising impact (i.e., the degree to which given advertisements are effective).

Relationship Marketing   A marketing practice involving the delivery of personalized attention, service, and support to target audiences in an effort to establish lasting bonds with customers, ensuring their enduring patronage.

Repositioning   The practice of altering the positioning characteristics of given product offerings in an effort to redefine the image associated with particular goods and services.

Retailer   An establishment that sells products directly to consumers.

Sales Concept   A marketing philosophy, prevalent during the mid-1900s, which emphasized salesmanship as a means of generating exchange, leading marketers to focus their attention on excellence in this area, typically at the expense of customers and their defined wants and needs.

Sales Promotion   A promotional method involving the use of incentives to stimulate customer interest. Examples include discount coupons, free gifts, samples, and contests.

Sales Representative   An individual employed by an organization to identify and contact customers in the marketplace who might have wants or needs for the goods and services offered by the employing establishment.

Segment   A group of individuals within a market who share common characteristics (e.g., age, income, tastes, preferences).

Segmentation The process of dividing a market into groups (i.e., segments) of individuals who share common characteristics. Segmentation, also termed *market segmentation*, is the first step of target marketing.

Seller Any party that offers products for sale to others.

Service An intangible product offering.

Social Marketing The use of marketing strategies and tactics to promote goods and services deemed to be beneficial to the health and well-being of individuals and society.

Substitute Product A product that differs from a particular offering but largely, and sometimes completely, fills equivalent wants and needs.

Supply Chain Management A marketing practice involving the comprehensive management of distribution networks to ensure efficient and effective business operations that will ultimately yield goods and services of significant value.

Target Market The name given to a market segment that has been selected (i.e., targeted) by an organization. Also referred to as a *target audience* or *target population*.

Target Marketing A three-step process that involves the division of a market into segments (i.e., market segmentation), the selection of attractive segments to pursue (i.e., targeting), and the determination of an appropriate and effective image for products to convey to customers (i.e., product positioning).

Targeting The selection of attractive market segments to pursue. Targeting is the second step of target marketing.

Television Advertising A form of electronic advertising that uses television (e.g., broadcast network television, cable television) to deliver promotional messages to target audiences.

Test Marketing A practice where marketers directly or indirectly seek consumer feedback regarding their new products by allowing target audiences to experience the offerings prior to full-scale marketplace introductions. Such experiences are offered to customers via product samples, trials, small-scale market releases, and other means.

Top-of-Mind Awareness   A marketing communications goal that refers to the first brands that come to mind when consumers think of products.

Transit Advertising   A form of outdoor advertising involving the use of public transportation vehicles (e.g., buses, taxis, trains) to display advertising messages to vehicular and pedestrian traffic in the course of their passenger transportation activities.

Unique Selling Proposition (USP)   A proposal forwarded to target audiences via an advertisement that touts the unique features and benefits possessed by a product offering for the purpose of attracting interest, attention, and exchange.

Value Added   A term that refers to the enhancements and improvements offered by given products that eclipse the features and benefits of current offerings in the market.

Vendor   Any party that carries a particular product offering and makes the item available to others for purchase and consumption.

Want   Something that is desired but not required for well-being and survival. A desire as opposed to a necessity.

Warehouse   (1) The act of storing goods for distribution or use at a later point in time. (2) A physical structure built for the purpose of storing goods for distribution or use at a later point in time.

Wearout   The tendency for the impact of an advertising message to diminish over time, necessitating that marketers periodically alter their advertising messages to ensure sustained impact.

Wholesaler   An intermediary in a channel of distribution that is situated between the producer of a product and the retailers that carry the particular offering.

Word-of-Mouth Publicity   Publicity generated via communications between and among peers regarding the benefits, or lack thereof, of given product offerings.

Zapping   A practice, undesirable to advertisers, where television viewers use their remote controls to change channels during commercial breaks, thus avoiding exposure to advertisements.

Index